THE RISE AND FALL OF THE FIRST GALACTIC EMPIRE: STAR WARS AND POLITICAL PHILOSOPHY

THE RISE AND FALL OF THE FIRST GALACTIC EMPIRE: STAR WARS AND POLITICAL PHILOSOPHY

MATEUSZ MACHAJ

DEDICATION

To all those who thunderously applaud real-world Sith lords

And to the memory of all those who refused to clap.

Acknowledgements

I thank Arkadiusz Sieroń, Matthew McCaffrey, and Jan Lewiński for their helpful comments. (However, they should remember: even though they are on the council of this project, I do not grant them the rank of master.) To my parents, and to my dear wife for her tolerance of my bizarre interests. Last but not least, I thank Luke, not the Skywalker, but my brother (such a Han Solo stan that he refuses to watch Episode VII), as he is responsible for my interest in both the social sciences and *Star Wars*. One of those ruined my life. I still don't know which one, but still: thanks, buddy!

The book was financed by independent, neutral systems in no way related to the resistance or the First Order. No Ewoks were harmed during production.

FOREWORD

Matthew McCaffrey
University of Manchester

It might seem easy to pass over a book like this. After all, countless authors write books applying serious ideas to seemingly unserious pop culture artefacts like *Star Wars*, so why should you care about this one? For three reasons: first, because this book is consistently clever; second, it's genuinely funny; and third, and most important, because its ideas *matter*.

Many people have written about the philosophical themes in *Star Wars*, and what they might mean for its fans in the real world. But in this book, Mateusz Machaj takes a fresh approach that sets his work apart within the genre. Rather than focus, for example, on the religious themes of the Force or the moral implications of humanity's relationship with technology, Machaj views the *Star Wars* saga as a parable about the dangers of political power. As he explains, each of the eight canonical films in the series adds its own insights into the nature of power and the corruption it breeds in society. When taken together, they offer a rich and fascinating narrative that weaves together ideas about commerce, social decline, politics, war, empire, and revolution. The films are just as much cautionary tales about the evils of political ambition as they are stories about family and personal redemption. Most of all, the *Star Wars* saga reveals how fragile are the freedoms and societies we hold dear.

Throughout each of the following chapters, Machaj draws on some of the key ideas of political philosophy and economics to explain the growth of power and what can be done to stop it. Yet the true originality of this book lies in the imagination Machaj uses to explain the political narrative: rather than stick to a few well-known scenes from the prequel trilogy, he takes his readers at light speed back and forth across the entire series of films, never missing an opportunity to draw a clever implication from the actions of a minor character or from a piece of throw-away dialogue. Sure, we know the Empire is evil, but what can the deleted scenes from *Return of the Jedi* tell us about the power of passive resistance to tyrannical government? Whether he's using Darth Vader's shifting definition of "the deal" to show the inherent flaws in the idea of social contract, or Boba Fett's bounty hunting to demonstrate how the economically inefficient Empire outsources to the private sector, he consistently finds unexpected ways to illustrate the simple wisdom of political philosophy.

Perhaps even more important, he does so with a relentless sense of humor. For Machaj, nothing in the universe is sacred, not even Jedi heroes like Qui-Gon Jinn, whose pseudoscience is compared to the anti-vaccination movement. The humor also extends far beyond the *Star Wars* universe, and careful readers will find many references to other films and TV series hidden throughout.

Finally, allow me to explain why a book like this—which seems to have an unserious topic—really matters. As Machaj shows, ideas can be infectious, and ideas about the dangers of power are always relevant and urgently needed, in the world today no less than at any other time in history. In an age of political corruption, war, and empire-building, ideas about peace and commerce must be spread far and wide. And one of the best ways to do that is through popular culture. As the late Roger Ebert explained, "The film philosophies that will live forever are the simplest-seeming ones. They may have profound depths, but their surfaces are as clear to an audience as a beloved old story." And that's why *Star Wars*— and this book—is so powerful: it appeals to a simple, shared cultural experience, which is exactly what makes it a perfect medium for spreading practical ideas about political philosophy. Just as *Star Wars* is timeless, so too are the ideas discussed in this book, which provide food for thought that we can only hope will be digested in less than a thousand years.

The book that follows is written with the kind of joyous fascination so many of us experienced when we first saw *Star Wars*, and that we have rediscovered countless times ever since. The author's passion is as contagious as the ideas he discusses. Ebert was surely thinking of a book like this when he wrote, "Those who analyze [*Star Wars*'s] philosophy do so, I imagine, with a smile in their minds. May the Force be with them."

CONTENTS

PREFACE: THERE IS SOMETHING IN *STAR WARS*

"It's like poetry. They rhyme."
— George Lucas

THIS is a story of the rise and fall of the First Galactic Empire, whose founding father was Palpatine. I am telling this story for future generations so they can understand that even something that happened a long time ago, in a galaxy far, far away may be extremely relevant to Earth's socio-political systems. The more we look into it, the more we see the world of *Star Wars* rhyming with our world. Sort of like poetry.

Many nonfiction *Star Wars* books already go beyond the simple adventure stories and teach us, on countless levels, something valuable about human beings. Some books concern religion and *Star Wars*, others philosophy and *Star Wars*, and so forth. What we lack though is a satisfying political account of the decline of the Old Republic and the rise of the Empire. My aim in this short book is to fill that gap. The magic of each of the seven episodes provides some key insights into how totalitarianism arises, and how it can be ultimately defeated.

I am going to start with an analysis of Palpatine's philosophical background, since every would-be political leader is a prisoner of some sort of ideological framework. Without understanding the background of his thinking, one can hardly understand his choices, motivations, and actions, besides simply labeling them evil. That label becomes too convenient: *Palpatine was evil. Besides, Palpatine was evil. He was behind all of this. Do you know why? Because he was evil.*

But we should do so much more than that in seeking to understand the sources of evil systems. Every dictator has had his views shaped by writers, thinkers, economists, ideologues, and philosophers. To fully comprehend a dictator and his political machine, one has to confront his particular inspirations. Understanding them also helps to see how various interrelated ideas may lead to the rise of dangerous dictatorial movements. Ultimately the history of mankind, like the history of all species in the galaxy, is a result of the clash of ideas. If the battle is to be won, and Palpatine's dictatorship to be avoided, it should be won in the intellectual ring: this is the only way to avoid a destructive armed conflict. Hence, our starting point is the origin of Palpatine's value system and his philosophical inspirations. Backed with his normative judgments, Palpatine put into action a well-thought-out plan for a hostile takeover of the galactic political system.

Movies are often treated as a lower form of art and entertainment than traditional styles like the novel. There are good reasons for this, as merely watching and listening are more passive than reading. While reading, we have to be more creative: we have to take a passage and "decode" it in our imagination. We're helping to build the world we're reading about. For this simple reason, diverse areas of our brain have to work much harder. No surprise then that books make us smarter—much more so than movies. Reading is like going to a brain gym: the brain is practicing so much harder than when we simply watch.

In watching movies, our attention is tied to something already defined in sight and sound. Not much can be added. Some things may be implied, but everything just goes along and appears in sequences automatically. But such experiences have their proper place in human life. Despite being "lower" forms of culture and less stimulating for the brain, movies and TV series are not to be thrown away. They still can be great forms of culture and very ambitious in depicting puzzling confrontations. This is possible even with very popular material.

I believe *Star Wars* to be an example. It comes off as a simplified adventure story of a young kid who, by a series of accidents, decides to save the galaxy—with a few complications along the way. I hope to convince you it may be seen as more than that. Even if not, *Star Wars* is simply a great excuse to talk about serious political and social issues. I am biased on this. To paraphrase one Nobel laureate in economics, everything I see and listen to makes me think about social systems. (The person added, "But I keep it out of the paper." Apparently, this advice is not working for me.)

Why *Star Wars*? Because it's a fairy tale told by and cooked up for adults (to some degree also for kids, but they do not grasp everything in it). One of the main components of its success is the wonderful creative design of the world (try watching most other sci-fi movies made in the seventies and see how much worse their visuals are). But what keeps it together is the story. Fairy tales are not just fanciful, made-up stories. They often contain valuable lessons about how things ought to be. Bedtime stories must offer something to be learned about good motives and appropriate choices. Why should anything be different for stories for adults, such as the *Star Wars* movies? Though they are mostly focused on the story, not the political system in which it happens, they nevertheless have something to say about political philosophy.

I have to apologize to all fans of the *Star Wars* expanded universe, none of which I will analyze here (despite my praise for books over movies in general).

The following book of course contains spoilers for Episodes I–VI. I assume readers have already watched those movies, since the goal is to discover some wisdom in them. If you have not seen them, then do so and come back to read afterward so that you won't be embarrassed for not knowing that the guy in the helmet is the kid's father.

If you're unsure about the picture of the bizarre-looking king on the cover, it comes from a very old book: *Leviathan*, by Thomas Hobbes. The king wishes to establish a unified political system over a whole territory to end anarchy in all forms. Palpatine's vision can be seen as Hobbesian, as I will discuss, though I do not at all plan to limit myself to just that element of Palpatine's thoughts and actions.

PART ONE: PHILOSOPHY OF PALPATINE

"I WILL MAKE IT LEGAL," OR "MY NAME IS PALPATINE AND I AM A GREEK SOPHIST"

WHETHER explicitly and with self-awareness or not, political leaders echo the ideas of past ideologues or philosophers. The famous economist John Maynard Keynes said this about economic ideas: "The ideas of economists and political philosophers, both when they are right and when they are wrong are more powerful than is commonly understood. Indeed, the world is ruled by little else. Practical men, who believe themselves to be quite exempt from any intellectual influences, are usually slaves of some defunct economist." This is no less true for the philosophical side of politics. More generally, we are all heirs of the ideas of past centuries, codified in books. Much like Molière's character who never realized that his whole life he'd been speaking prose, we are unintentionally adhering to some specific philosophy or repeating some economist's ideas when we comment about social reality.

What kind of tradition in moral philosophy does Palpatine represent? No doubt we should place him with the Greek Sophists. Perhaps oversimplifying a bit, the main dichotomy in Greek moral philosophy was between Socrates's camp and the Sophists'. Socrates argued that good is objective and is a universal standard in human life. We may want to point out that he became famous for his Socratic method of questioning everything and inviting everyone to think. How come we should associate this questioning guy with the idea of objective good and truth? His approach was not to overthrow everything. He believed questioning leads to wisdom, and wisdom allows us to fully discover what good and justice are. The Socratic way of always questioning assumptions is nowadays often associated with the critical rationalism of Karl Popper, an Austrian philosopher who emphasized that there should be no dogmas in science. Such an idea is a feature of most advanced philosophical seminars. Do you think we should believe in something just because some authority stated the case? It just ain't so.

Phrasing a query properly is itself a step in the search for answers. Socrates went on: As questioning leads to growth in knowledge, an educated man is capable of discovering and recognizing what goodness is. He somewhat wrongly believed that knowledge automatically leads to proper choices, and that one cannot be wise and evil at the same time. Crucially then, he held an objective view of moral philosophy and believed in humans' potential to discover truths by critically examining what is right and what is wrong.

Sophists, on the other hand, rejected such a Socratic path. Their rejection was especially noticeable in their description of the law in relation to the idea of goodness and justice. For Sophists, discovery of goodness does not have to lead to proper choices, but more importantly, the concept of goodness itself is very fuzzy.

Can law—a set of rules organizing society—be good, fair, just? The two most prominent Sophists were Thrasymachus and Critias. Both of them questioned the foundations of Socratic moral philosophy and distrusted his moralism, but for different reasons. For Thrasymachus, might is justice: *Listen—I say that justice is nothing other than the advantage of the stronger.* If one has enough force and strength to exercise his or her power and impose it onto the rest, then the mightiness becomes justness. Almost tautologically, whoever wins is the ultimate Mr. or Ms. Justice—a Judge Dredd shouting, "I am the law."

For Critias on the other hand, might is not really justice, but justice is simply a charade by the mighty to make it look like their rule is justified by philosophy. Critias and Thrasymachus took rather different routes based on totally different foundations that led to similar nihilist practical conclusions. For Critias, the concept of justice in general is just an invention of the rulers. Nothing like it exists objectively. Successful rule requires control and efficient management. But the whole idea of legal philosophy means to not only govern the people by force, but use rhetoric to convince the people that the system is just. Hence the moral code is invented as propaganda and to reassure the public that the rules imposed upon them should not be questioned, since they flow from some form of rightness. In other words, lecturing the people about what is good serves as a social spell to make them quiet: Don't question the order. Accept it and abide by it.

The views of Critias and Thrasymachus concern distinct concepts of goodness and law. Even so, they lead to similar attacks on moralism. Are you making arguments about how the law represents goodness, justice, and fairness? Thrasymachus would say: Do not be silly. What you call goodness is always equal to whatever the rules, implemented by brute force, say. The rules are always good in themselves, no matter how bad they seem. Critias would say with somewhat more sophistication: Do not be silly. What you call goodness is simply propaganda, a social spell to calm everyone down and suppress social unrest.

Either way—whether we say "Strongness equals goodness" or "Goodness is fake"—we end up with nihilism: denying a moralistic approach to assessing the law. As a result, legal and political reality is awful, as the horrid tricks in *House of Cards* or the fights in *Game of Thrones* demonstrate nicely. Moralism in the legal order? Now, as Michael Corleone put it, who's being naïve, Kay?

Is nihilism the only option? Are things really that bad? Must we lose all hope? Say what you want about the tenets of Socratic innocence, at least they're an ethos. Surely so, but the unfortunate reality of political battles in the real world or on good TV shows is not something invented by our imagination. It is very hard to remain optimistic about finding goodness in existing legal systems. What we often witness is simply brute force.

How does this relate to *Star Wars* and to Palpatine? Obviously, he doesn't stand on Socrates's side. He doesn't believe moralism plays any role in political and legal controversies. Nor is he interested in reflecting on what it means to govern and how rule becomes legitimate. He belongs with the most nihilistic of all the Sophists. How would he have reacted to disputes about the rightness of a particular political system? He would have shrugged.

For example, while discussing the invasion of the planet Naboo, a representative of the Trade Federation suggested that perhaps the recommended option—to attack—was unlawful:

"Ah, my lord, is that ... legal?"

"I will make it legal."

Notice the phrasing: he will *make* it legal. Socrates would say: *I will find out whether it is legal.* For Socrates, the world needs to be understood, observed so that things around us may be discovered, including the morality of our actions. The general rule applies well to all parts of human life. Why should a legal system be any different?

Naturally, to Palpatine, the law is not to be discovered, because then the law would bind us and severely constrain our ambitious plans. Moreover, besides functioning as a potential constraint, the law does not represent anything moral. It is just a convention that can be bent for the goals we choose. The law doesn't reflect anything more than artificial rules based on words, only an obstacle to completing our projects. Law does not come from any Socratic reflection on how the world really works.

You are worried about something being illegal? Not a problem. We can easily make it legal. It's not time to think. It's time to act. Perhaps the sad thing about modern reality is that politicians are not very far away from Palpatine. Whenever any need arises for taking action, they tend to treat the law as a tool, not a reflection of universal ideas for creating peace.

By following in the footsteps of the Sophists and denying moralism, Palpatine is participating in another tradition: legal positivism.

"I AM THE SENATE ... IT'S TREASON, THEN," OR "MY NAME IS PALPATINE, AND I DO NOT BELIEVE IN NATURAL LAW"

THE idea that law is a necessary device in social life is a powerful and brilliant invention for developing a general framework for everyday living—often not directly visible, but always having a direct impact on how people get along. Without such a nexus of rules, civilization could not exist. Yet most of us believe that rules are not necessarily just. Following Socrates's path, we believe law has to be something more than simply technical rules like those in a board game. This line of thinking led to the development of the natural-law tradition, in which there is much more to understanding the law than just looking at technicalities. The tradition is associated with scholars of the Middle Ages, especially Hugo Grotius. In referring to something external to the set of rules, natural-law thinkers were inspired by religion and the concept of God as something universal, eternal, absolutely fair and just—an ideal perhaps unreachable in human life, but understandable on some metaphysical level. The real world can be awful, but we have this ideal to which we can refer, the story goes.

Yet the tradition did not only have a religious basis. The argument made by Grotius was actually that natural law, the law governing an eternal and universal order, was something to be rationally understood and intellectually (not just spiritually) appraised. Even though the natural-law tradition was ignited with a religious spark and exploded by searching for a divine role in human existence, natural law itself was to be revealed by reason. From the start, the tradition of natural law developed a path away from religious dogma, thus creating its future as a standalone discipline—much like the sciences in general. Natural law and its offspring, natural rights, are to be given to human beings, whether created by God or not, by virtue of being human. Many natural-rights thinkers believe that the metaphysical question of who or what made humans is not essential to explaining why people have inalienable rights.

To complicate the matter, human morality was subjected to biological evolution. Therefore, it changed and became radically different across societies (and was not universal for very long). Yet such a subjectivist historical perspective does not invalidate the idea that a rational and empathic reflection on what individual rights each person deserves is possible.

In any case, natural-law thinkers stated that something lies above the written laws of human beings, the so-called positive law, or the set of rules that arrived on Earth by the will of rulers. Natural-law thinkers believed that to be legitimate, rules have to come from the "natural" order of things. On the other side of the spectrum, there is the positivist approach to law (legal positivism), well summarized by the Forrest Gumpian expression: law is what law does. It is nothing more.

What do this mean? The term "positive" in the social sciences usually refers to a descriptive analysis, describing how the social world works. Positive statements abstract from values and various normative programs of how to organize social life. To put it differently, they do not tell us how things ought to be, but simply how they are and how they could be (not *should be*). It's just like medical science: it doesn't directly tell you to take care of your life and stop eating junk food; it merely stipulates that if you don't, then the long-term health consequences will be serious. Legal positivism is a critical and productive jurisprudential tradition of analyzing how legal rules actually function, without going much into the question of how things should be. But somewhere over the rainbow of analyzing those legal peculiarities is the reflection that law is just a convention, a structure of words assigning social roles to various groups and individuals.

Where does Palpatine fit into this picture? He is the master of legal positivism. For him, laws are merely the rules of a game. In contrast to this perspective, the idea of natural law opened the door for justifying civil disobedience. Think about it: if there is such a thing as natural law that can be discovered by human reason and that is more important than the will of any particular human being, then it may happen that rules break the natural law and therefore deserve to be ignored or overthrown—much like how Henry David Thoreau advised revolt against oppressive government. If, on the other hand, nothing exists besides positive law, nothing beyond the arbitrary rules of the game, then we can play with the rules as we like without facing any limits.

Rulers are always scary and dangerous. They hold big swords or guns. They have a legal monopoly over a certain territory. Obviously, these circumstances create a potential threat to the public. Knowing of this threat, Enlightenment philosophers—especially Montesquieu and John Locke, both from the natural-law tradition—developed the concept of separation of powers. All powers in the legal system should not be held by one person or one particular agency; otherwise, great dangers to the liberties of the people await.

Similar thinking led to the creation of constitutions. The philosophical spirit behind the ideas of constitutions and the separation of powers is that the watchmen can be watched if they do not control every part of the legal structure. In theory, such limitations can work smoothly. In practice, their efficacy varies, and often real-world separation of powers is deficient.

I intentionally use the word "spirit," as Montesquieu wrote about the "spirit of the law." In the legal structure, separation of powers and constitutions are also conventions. The natural-law sympathizer would believe them to reflect some important ideas of justice. Natural-law deniers would simply view them as a map directing them on how to move in the game of politics. Palpatine takes the second position and very consciously uses the existing rules to take over all of the main branches of the government. Is he doing this *against the law*? Not really:

his actions could be seen as legal. Is he doing this *against the spirit of the law?* Yes.

Consider a famous anecdote about Kurt Gödel, the brilliant logician who devised the so-called incompleteness theorem. In a very watered-down version, the idea is that any mathematical system cannot be complete and that every system is limited in terms of what it covers. Gödel applied for US citizenship. During the application, he had to answer some basic questions about the American political system. The talk focused in part on the Constitution and dictatorship. The government official hinted of the evils of dictatorship in Germany and glowed with satisfaction that such would not happen in the United States because the Constitution acts as a safeguard. Gödel, however, responded that he could prove that dictatorship is possible under the American system. The Constitution, as a convention, cannot fully rule out that possibility.

Palpatine could only applaud such an observation. In each step of his plan, Palpatine modifies the existing positive law by gaining more and more powers. In the end, he is granted supreme powers that free him from the separation of powers and the central tenets of the "constitution." The change does not happen because of a revolutionary uprising or military takeover. It happens through legal means. Other powers willingly abdicate, and the constitution is modified by the people in charge—all according to the rules of the game. The positive law is almost perfectly respected, although the spirit of the law is not—nor is natural law.

The Emperor simply does not care about the spirit of law. For him it does not exist, which makes him part of the opposition to the natural-law tradition. He declares that he is the senate, but not because of some military coup. He is the senate because the senate decides he should take its place. He himself is the constitution, because various legal measures were undertaken to change the constitution, procedures allowed for in the constitution itself. Anyone denying his rights acts against the existing positive law. That is why arresting him might be an act of treason. And for what crime? Being a Sith lord? Come on: the Republic guaranteed religious freedom, right? Windu, you demagogue!

Resisting the Emperor on a purely conventional level may be problematic. Maybe certain rules could undermine plans to create the Empire. But much more promising is the tradition of placing limitations upon power itself. Lord Acton beautifully commented that "power corrupts, and absolute power corrupts absolutely." That is why the government must always be constrained by various checks and balances. By abolishing those checks and balances, the spirit of the law is overthrown too. Surely some ways can make that spirit more concrete in the form of specified and written rules. But as Gödel showed us, nothing can be completely predetermined in our systems of thought. The legal framework is no different. That is why some fundamental human values always take precedence over any existing legal proceedings, since ideas determine the course of the world in the long run.

In discussing Palpatine's approach to the law, I should mention another important thinker: the French economist Frédéric Bastiat. He was the author of an inspiring pamphlet called *The Law*, which lies firmly in the natural-law tradition. Bastiat started off with a strong cry: "The law perverted! And the police powers of the state perverted along with it! The law, I say, not only turned from its proper purpose but made to follow an entirely contrary purpose! The law become the weapon of every kind of greed! Instead of checking crime, the law itself guilty of the evils it is supposed to punish!"

Does this happen in Palpatine's rise to power? It is reasonable to think so. The law as a social tool became in the rotten Republic only the means to pervert the very idea of law as a means of achieving peace and harmony. Defending Palpatine's view is only possible if one believes there is no more to humanity than flesh, bones, atoms, and animal-like customs. Palpatine really couldn't care less about peace and harmony. From a purely legal point of view, he is the senate. But is there any place in his regime for such values as goodness, fairness, and justice, or is

Palpatine a total nihilist believing that only aggression brings social balance?

"GOODNESS IS A POINT OF VIEW," OR
"NIETZSCHE IS MY INSPIRATION"

IN a very climatic, though somewhat disappointing scene, Palpatine prods Anakin Skywalker to turn to the Dark Side. The scene is well directed and even convincingly acted on both sides, but lacks the intellectual rigor we would expect from Palpatine: he could more fluently and powerfully refute Anakin's childish claims of the Jedi's apparent goodness. Despite such disappointment, we get more clues on whom Palpatine is following aside from the Sophists and legal positivists: Friedrich Nietzsche.

Nietzsche famously said, "God is dead," but that was not just a simple declaration. It was something more: a frontal attack on the typical moralist framework, on universal good, or on any of the eternal values and goals present in ideological and religious systems. There is no other world besides the one we live in. There is only the here and now, nothing else. Therefore, one can either stand and fight for his goals, or simply move to the side and stay in pitiful conditions, worshipping some other world that in reality has no bearing on us. For some, such a perspective can be broadly seen as another form of nihilism, but with Nietzsche this is not necessarily the case. His point was actually to reject the previous moral standards that cherished the afterlife or some form of outside-world valuation.

What is left for us after such rejection? A Nietzschean "will to power." Do what you feel, stand up for yourself, do not shy away from your goals—which should be the prime target of your considerations, not balance, not eternal peace, not the lives of others. Your life is the most important thing about you, and it should be at the center of your choices and values. In a very general sense, such theses can of course be found even in the systems we consider altruistic. Christianity, for example, is also based on individualism, as only a particular person can receive salvation—not the group, not the family, not the nation, but a particular human being. A person is baptized, a person receives Holy Communion, and so forth. In any case, despite some individualistic flavor, Christianity is miles apart from Nietzsche's philosophy, because Christianity teaches that human beings are something more than creatures of the existing world. Nietzsche, on the other hand, would say it is almost a slave's illusion to believe that people possess a dual nature. Human beings are creatures of the existing world and should search for the best goal right here, right now. Hence, even though both systems refer to self-interest, they define "self-interest" by using different metaphysical standards. In the end, they are polar opposites, but they both rely on quasi-egoistic reasoning. After all, practically every single ideological system tries to tell you what is in your best interest, right?

Another problem with differing paths of individualism is that nothing is completely individualistic and detached from society. Clearly drawn lines for personal choices exist due to the necessity of social interaction. Not everything is permitted in many individualistic philosophies that are secular—for example, various forms of liberalism. How is it with Nietzsche? Where is the line to be drawn? Nietzsche does not really give us an answer. The "will to power" became a code name for ambition and a call for courageous actions to clear potential obstacles to the envisioned goal. Palpatine's tease perfectly reflects such an attitude: *My dear Anakin, what could be more important than Padme's life? What could be more important than your personal happiness with her? Focus on your feelings, as they will naturally guide you to the goal you desire. Did our green friend (Yoda) really tell you to just let go? Save her at all cost!*

In one of the most startling scenes of the TV series *Breaking Bad*, the corrupt and immoral character Walter White offers a stunning quote about how to mute one's conscience: "When we do what we do for good reasons, then we've got nothing to worry about. And there's no better reason than family." The end justifies the means. I can almost see White sitting at the bar with Anakin explaining his reasoning: "Just close your eyes, and tell yourself you do it for your family. Killing those younglings would be much easier to do."

Pop versions of philosophy are often problematic, and such is the case with the Force. There is, however, one important difference between the Dark Side and the proper way to use the Force: rational reflection. The Force invites rationality into the mysterious reflection upon the world and our choices. Sit down, drink some coffee, relax, get the bad feelings out of your head, and reflect. What is really important besides your temporary passions? When you forget that anger toward your neighbor, what is it that really matters? When you think about death and the afterlife, what do you want your legacy to be?

The Dark Side, on the other hand, does not invite rationality. Or perhaps when it invites rational thinking, it is to add fuel to temporary emotions. Your thinking is not based on an external and universal perspective on your choices. The famous Kantian rule in ethics is to act as if you would like your action to inform a general rule for everyone. Such thinking is achieved by the philosopher who is calm, well read, and aware of the existence of other human beings. There even must be some compassion or empathy. But Nietzsche and Palpatine could hardly care less: *Get Grandpa Kant out of the way. No time for your intellectual mumbo jumbo. Now I need to take action, because otherwise I will lose what is most important in my life. There is only this life, a fragile one that may quickly disappear. Kant is for losers needing excuses, Nietzsche is for winners, and winners do not complain.*

But temporary emotions stand in the way of calm and intellectual thinking about oneself. Any logical operations are there to rationalize ex post whatever our emotions make us do. As human beings we are naturals at this. No matter how bad our choices are (according to some standard we might believe in), we can easily justify them somehow. One interpretation of Nietzsche is that he would gladly clap for this fact. The will to power has to prevail over doubt

In the end, the will to power is what separates the morality of masters from the morality of slaves, another dichotomy in Nietzsche's system. Purportedly, slaves praise their weakness, sickness, and poverty, just like Christians do. They try to find eternal values, whereas in reality they are the lost fight and invent a system to feel better about their misery. Masters, on the other hand, praise winning, conquest, and strength. Moralities differ because they are a way to rationalize the conditions in which persons live and also their choices readily available. Once the master takes complete charge through his will to power, he gets on the path to becoming an *Übermensch*—a superhuman who rejects all past moral values based on good and evil. He chooses to go "beyond good and evil" and cherish present life in itself by throwing away any idea of sacrifice because it would mean falling for the pitiful morality of slaves.

All these basic concepts fit quite well into Palpatine's thinking, and they also influence Anakin, who is not only metaphorically a slave, but also literally. Freed from his chains, he wants to fully develop his powers and skills to extend his influence in the present life. His passions become even more negative when he realizes his beloved Padme must die. That is why relentless and fast action is necessary. Unfortunately, the Jedi stand in the way and hold him back (even at some point humiliating him). *Do not do this, do not do that. Now is not the right time. When the time comes, you will know.* On top of that, some of the Jedi masters treat him like a child and openly show him disrespect. They are poor teachers and terrible mentors. It all becomes too much when Anakin hears he should be happy about his wife's death even before the tragedy occurs. Who would not go crazy with this type of advice about how to save a dying wife?

How do I save my love?

You do not. Just be happy she is dead.

What? Yoda, did you really say that?

Palpatine cleverly suggested to Anakin that other routes were possible. He did not even have to rely on manipulation. He needed only to refer to emotions. Just do what you feel is necessary, and do not hesitate, for hesitation is a sign of weakness. Good depends on your point of view, as everyone has his or her own values, as Nietzsche would tell us. It is up to you to choose your way of living: as a slave, or as a master. If someone refuses to grant you the rank of master, he wants you to remain a slave. Your responsibility is to take a stand against him, even if he is a well-respected Jedi. So we see the Jedi are no different than anyone else in a republic. They are on their own path to power too.

The title of one of Nietzsche's works is *Beyond Good and Evil*. Anakin is encouraged by Palpatine to move beyond those simple and at times ambiguous concepts. To defend a Nietzschean perspective, one could argue that reference to good and evil has often been used by rulers to justify their rule over the majority of the population (remember Critias?). There is some form of sophism at work in the concepts referring back to various moral philosophies. For example, terrorists can also attempt to justify their actions with reference to eternality and universal goodness, so Nietzsche did have a very relevant practical point.

Nietzsche was not really a nihilist and did not support the fascists, as has been claimed (the last of his major works was published posthumously and was edited by his sister, who was a Hitler supporter). He appears to have believed that by philosophically undermining all previous moral systems, he would prepare the ground for a discussion of meta-ethics by intellectuals focused on developing humankind. There is, however, too much hope in such a strategy. To paraphrase a prominent quote: it is easy to remove the notion of absolute morality from thinking, but the vacant space hardly ever stays unoccupied. In other words, by abolishing the quest for the ultimate truth and ethical values, we are paving the way for someone functioning as the ultimate value without any moral background. (That is how human minds tend to function: they put things into named boxes. Hardly anyone can manage to dodge this practice.) Hence, even though Nietzsche should definitely not be seen as a nihilist (sorry, Hollywood), in practice he can be seen as having started a nihilist party.

Anakin's moving away from fixed concepts of good and evil leads him to fully develop his will to power, to strive to bring more things under his control. Palpatine brilliantly pushes him along this path. Almost like the devil, who gladly takes the chance to emphasize human freedom, he says you should free yourself from those chains and you care primarily about yourself. Go pursue your goals, for there is nothing valuable besides them. Then comes a twist in the justification: do it, because, paradoxically, you are predetermined to do it. So Nietzsche was immediately replaced in favor of something else. This should come as no surprise though, as it is very typical for a politician to selectively take from others what they find suitable for achieving their horrid goals.

"IT IS YOUR DESTINY. EVERYTHING IS PROCEEDING AS I HAVE FORESEEN," OR "WELCOME TO THE WORLD OF HISTORICAL NECESSITY"

So far we have considered Palpatine's views on legal philosophy, ethics, and politics. Much remains to be said about his views on the philosophy of history. How is history shaped? Does it depend on particular choices? Or are some mysterious historical forces stronger than individual choices? Is history uncertain and shaped ultimately by human action, or by some much more deterministic forces?

Palpatine clearly seems to have adhered to the deterministic view. First, he claims to have foreseen exactly how things would develop. This concerns both Anakin's transformation and his son's inescapable fate. Anakin falls for this narrative when he asks Luke to join them—claiming the Emperor foresaw this. Second, Palpatine strongly emphasizes the concept of destiny. One is destined to do things. There is little scope for human choice, as the delicately designed web of conditions creates for us paths that somehow we have to follow because there are no sensible alternatives. The Emperor is of course the master in framing such inescapable choices (which ironically places him outside the deterministic web).

This kind of view necessarily moves us toward the notion of historical determinism. It is Wilhelm Friedrich Hegel whose ideas had to accompany Palpatine in explaining why Sith rule could not be avoided— almost as if one were to claim it was necessary for the Bolsheviks to destroy Russia and for the Nazis to take over Germany. In the case of communist rule, there were thousands of pages inspired by Marx, who built a whole socioeconomic theory describing basic material forces that organize cultural and social life. Yet the forces are constantly moving, leading to strong tensions within society. As those contradictions pile up—the story goes—the forces finally lead to huge shifts that unavoidably produce communist utopia: the place where all human problems are ultimately solved. A Marxist would say he is sure the contradictions will materialize no matter what. We can even just sit back, have a drink, and wait for the inevitable. Yes, I know, the hypocrites were doing precisely the opposite.

One of the greatest critics of deterministic views of history was Karl Popper, who called these views "historicism": the notion that some mysterious (Hegelian) forces determine the course of events and people just have to accept this as fact. The fallacious idea of preset sequences of events was so strongly used to justify the creation of various totalitarian regimes that Popper even dedicated his book to the victims of historicism: "In memory of the countless men and women of all creeds or nations or races who fell victim to the fascist and communist belief in Inexorable Laws of Historical Destiny."

In the history of various totalitarian implementations of utopian visions, a common problem is identifying the ultimate goal. The precise character of the ultimate goal can vary to a great extent. And people from various sides are ready to kill because they have different interpretations of what the ultimate goal really is. The Second Coming of Jesus? The triumph of materialism? Worldwide communism? *Lebensraum* for the *Übermensch*? You choose it (and you can stay comfortable unless it is you who is being taken to the concentration camp). Whether a political party or a sectarian religious figure, the leaders share the ultimate-goal trick. What a great piece of propaganda and call to action. Notice that mainstream religions also talk about the eventual ending, from which the discipline of eschatology develops, but they do not provide the date and the specifics like extreme ideologues do (one of the main differences). Contrary to the sects and parties, they find deep meaning in not providing the exact date (for example, that of the Messiah's return), and therefore human choice is still at the center of their philosophy.

For historicism, the goal becomes the most important thing—more than any human being, more than the means. Any means are justified, for not only is the goal important, it is also the only possible thing that can materialize in the future. Ironically, from a practical point of view, adherents of such extreme doctrines also believe in choice. The ultimate goal is to provide an opium for the masses, a tool to mobilize the crowd to give support and perhaps exercise violence to sustain the wicked rulers. Despite their wickedness, debating their status and nature in terms of values is beside the point. They are here, and they signify how powerful historical laws are. Resistance is futile, so you'd better join or you'll be destroyed. If you are not with me, then you are my enemy. In any case, dictators tend to emphasize that things have to be their way. How is there method in such madness? People fairly quickly realize that totalitarian regimes are nasty. Dictators need to constantly refer to historical necessity to remind the people they have no alternative.

All the rhetoric Palpatine uses fits nicely into such a Hegelian deterministic narrative. My dear Anakin, do not be fooled. Your will to power acts like gravity toward the goal. There is no other way to create balance and peace in the Republic.

Naturally, contrary to deterministic claims, history is shaped by people's choices and the ideas they cherish, as is proven to Palpatine when young Skywalker shows him one can make a moral choice even in the most dire circumstances. We will come back to this point in describing how empires fall.

Before we move on to another disciple of Palpatine, one should note Hegel's approach to the political order and the state. As in the case of Nietzsche, he was not an evil thinker justifying rulers' torture and killing of citizens. He did not favor a totalitarian order. Nevertheless, Hegel greatly romanticized rulers. The laws of history are based on contradictions because there is one spirit guiding and developing society. The government is a manifestation of this spirit. His positive feelings about political centralization are reflected well in the following quote: "I saw the Emperor—this world-soul—riding out of the city on reconnaissance. It is indeed a wonderful sensation to see such an individual, who, concentrated here at a single point, astride a horse, reaches out over the world and masters it." Yes, the word "emperor" is really in there, though Hegel did not mean Palpatine, because then the quote would have to have contained the phrase "astride a speeder."

Since we are talking about political centralization, we cannot forget the decisive political philosopher for Palpatine: Thomas Hobbes.

"I WILL NOT LET THIS REPUBLIC BE SPLIT IN TWO," OR "PALPATINE UNDERSTANDS THOMAS HOBBES WELL"

PALPATINE is a political centralist. He has to be. Without political centralism, the monopolization of power is impossible. Without a big state, how can one impose a Sith-dominated centralistic order? That would be unmanageable. In the first three episodes of the *Star Wars* saga, Palpatine is constantly struggling to stop other regions from seceding from the Republic (all while employing a powerful double agent in their midst). When you think about it, all political leaders and systems are to some extent centralistic, for they impose their laws on all provinces within their territory. This leads to various political tensions and internal conflicts, sometimes even to civil wars. The creators of *Star Wars* actually did not portray Palpatine's views as something inherently negative, because perhaps they did not think Palpatine is wrong here. They also believed in the idea of keeping one big republic. Why? They give no sensible answer. We will talk more about this in later sections.

For now, we should turn to another colossal figure of political philosophy to explain Palpatine's position on the importance of centralized power. Ultimately, this discussion is about the most fundamental question in the history of ideas: who is to govern, and why? Who get to be watchmen? The vast majority of political doctrines—except for some anarchist ones—are based on the idea that only a state can provide social order. Whether we're talking about classical liberalism, conservatism, socialism, communism, or social democracy, they all start the same way: only the state can provide law and order. Otherwise we are to have total chaos, the war of all against all, where life is brutal, nasty, and short.

Dominant political doctrines owe a lot to Thomas Hobbes, a British philosopher who used the concept of a war of all against all to explain the state of nature occupied by human beings. In the state of nature, people are not peaceful savages, noble countrymen, but are like beasts and animals fighting for territory and the resources necessary for survival. The only way peace is possible is through creating an ultimate sovereign—the state, the law, the final judge—which in the end decides who is right and who is wrong. Then the fighting can finally stop, and people can enter some other occupation than fighting.

Hobbes had empirical reasons to believe this to be true, as he witnessed the consequences of a ghastly civil war in England that resulted in thousands of unnecessary deaths and terrors. All this because people could not agree on who was to rule, who should win the "game of thrones." In a way, one could see a Hobbesian understanding of the government-led order not as an alternative to total anarchy. Rather, government is a natural product of anarchy, because in anarchy people are struggling, fighting, and gathering into armies to impose their rule on others. No rules are binding, no legal proceeding settled, and everything can be questioned, including your basic rights, freedom, life, and property—unless some ultimate ruler imposes order on others so that finally there will be peace because competition for the higher power is over. Eventually someone will win it.

I may be twisting Hobbes's thought a little bit, because he did offer some form of dichotomy between anarchy and state. He attempted a thought experiment, as he argued that the state is created in a somewhat voluntary manner. Of course, no state in the history of the world was created voluntarily. They virtually always evolved from making weaker people submit to new rulers. Yet the Hobbesian thought experiment is the following: brutish things are in the nature of human beings, but if we were offered a choice between war and an ultimate sovereign, then we would mostly choose the second alternative to finally live without that war of all against all, which in the end would produce a sovereign anyway. The winner may be a thug, but it is better to have a recognized, predictable thug than to constantly roll the dice and risk getting a worse one. Hence, instead of abolishing the government, or overthrowing it, let us just accept it, for it is necessary in a stable society. Revolutions can abolish rulers, but other rulers will come along eventually. The jobs of state officials hardly stay vacant for any length of time. The way they rise from anarchy may be very painful. Every social change is unpredictable, as is the case with overthrowing the rulers.

The paradoxical nature of Hobbes's reasoning is that it is inconsequential. On the one hand, it clearly follows that the rulers are bad people like those in *Game of Thrones*. Someone has to win the crown. And we'd better accept them, or endure further wars. Does it really make it an agreement? We may say that the state and rules exist *as if* there is an agreement between the rulers and population (which of course is never the case). The ruler is the lesser evil, because the alternative is total war. Once a reign is established, a proper question can be raised: how do you question it? What if the government is doing something we do not accept, either for moral or simple practical reasons? Can we cancel the contract? Hobbes's response was, of course, "No way":[1]

> First, because they covenant, it is to be understood they are not obliged by former covenant to anything repugnant hereunto. And consequently they that have already instituted a Commonwealth, being thereby bound by covenant to own the actions and judgments of one, cannot lawfully make a new covenant amongst themselves to be obedient to any other, in anything whatsoever, without his permission. And therefore, they that are subjects to a monarch cannot without his leave cast off monarchy and return to the confusion of a disunited multitude; nor transfer their person from him that beareth it to another man, other assembly of men: for they are bound, every man to every man, to own and be reputed author of

---

[1] There is one exception for Hobbes: if the ruler does not provide safety and therefore conditions under his rule are as horrible as under anarchy.

all that already is their sovereign shall do and judge fit to be done; so that any one man dissenting, all the rest should break their covenant made to that man, which is injustice: and they have also every man given the sovereignty to him that beareth their person; and therefore if they depose him, they take from him that which is his own, and so again it is injustice. Besides, if he that attempted to depose his sovereign be killed or punished by him for such attempt, he is author of his own punishment, as being, by the institution, author of all his sovereign shall do; and because it is injustice for a man to do anything for which he may be punished by his own authority, he is also upon that title unjust.

In other words: consent for the contract with the state is not necessary. It is always assumed that the individual has no choice but to accept it. Hardly sounds like a true contract, right? Vader's wonderful retort to Lando Calrissian is actually an excellent explanation of how the supposed social contract with government works: "I am altering the deal. Pray I don't alter it any further." In such a Hobbesian perspective, no one has the right to secede from the Sith's Leviathan state and its monopoly on galactic governance. Palpatine is a pure Hobbesian in the flesh, and he will not let the Republic be split. Why not? Because he wants unlimited power. Freedom to secede, even peacefully, threatens his dictatorial project. With freedom of provinces to secede, power cannot be unlimited.

"Once again, the Sith will rule the galaxy, and we shall have peace." What a wonderful quote from the Emperor. There is nothing untrue in it. After all, everyone—without exception—wants peace. The quarrels come from disagreements on the conditions for peace. Hitler and Stalin wanted peace. So does Palpatine, who is strongly interested in ending all those silly conflicts, first with the separatists, then with the rebellion. Let us just stop the meaningless resistance in any form and create one big galactic state with one universal Hobbesian ruler in order to prevent any conflicts.

Hobbes's thinking was reflected in the minds of most politicians in

Star Wars. In this way the saga mirrors real-world politics, as most governments are quite interested in keeping full control over their monopolies. Governments are hardly willing at any time to give away their prerogatives or refrain from gaining more—especially when the consequences of doing so sound so horrifying: let us keep our absolute monopoly, or we are all going to kill each other. Precisely this threat is presented to the Galactic Senate, and so it gives away special powers to the supreme chancellor. We have to be submissive, the Hobbesian-Palpatinean story goes, because society is so full of evil people just waiting to trigger a deadly war of all against all. All we have to do to secure ourselves from such disastrous consequences is to pick one of those people and offer them all possible powers. And we shall have peace. Yet as another philosopher said: *Yeah, well, you know, that's just, like, your opinion, Hobbes.*

"Always two there are. No more, no less," or "One Sith to rule them all"

WE have to mention a logical and significant attribute of our dear emperor—an attribute not arising from major studies of philosophy, but from sociology and realpolitik. I mean here the famous Sith rule: there can only be two Sith, no more, no less. Why there can't be less than two is easy to explain: There must be continuity. One Sith is a huge risk. If killed, the whole tradition is lost, so there needs to be more if their quest for power is to be carried on. Why though do we have to stop at two and not expand the group further? Isn't it better to have a broader school plotting and conspiring so the Sithian tradition could flourish even further?

The answer lies in the exact nature of the Sithian idea of social order: it has to be closed, hierarchical, and monopolistic. A plan to watch over and direct everyone requires full obedience, no dialogue, no internal competition. A couple of heads rarely create an obvious and universally accepted consensus that can be planned from the very beginning. Whenever we have several people with similar intellectual capabilities, a spontaneous process is being started. Who knows what may come of that? Discussion, questioning, quarrelling, even fighting. Think about any thriving tradition or institution, whether in thought, art, sports, or science. It can be your favorite rock band, maybe one that had problems with staying together for a long time. Or a wonderful dream team in sports. Rich traditions are not homogenous, because people are different (hooray for that!). Differences are present among people on the same level, but they also develop across levels. Each student tries to build on what the teacher has done because most systems are evolving. Yet in order to develop, it is almost necessary to question what was once accepted as a standard. Developing traditions means also eroding them by undermining past ideas—at least to some extent.

Now imagine having many people in similar positions, with similar powers and capabilities. Because of their heterogeneity, there's room for colliding ideas and sometimes major differences of opinion. Most developed societies have certain ways of handling this: reasoning and discussing without the necessity to use physical force. Relying on intellectual reflection and sensible human communication is the cornerstone of doing good business with one another. The problem is that Sith rule is not based on reason and Socratic discussions. Sith are driven by passions, emotions, strong reactions, and unquestionable devotion to one ultimate goal. Under such a strict system of values, blind obedience becomes the best virtue, whereas reflecting, questioning, discussing are only means to creating unnecessary obstacles. The point is to win, not to stand in your own way. Any reflection upon tactics merely postpones the inevitable. And remember, the inevitable is coming in the Hegelian manner. Did you forget that everything transpires according to Palpatine's desire?

The ultimate goal we mentioned before requires a homogenous and loyal group of soldiers. The iron law of oligarchy, associated with sociologist Robert Michels, observes simply that most groups develop into oligarchical structures, in which a group of leaders decides about the future state of the group. It is neither completely democratic, where everyone decides to the same extent, nor completely monarchical, where just one person decides. Michels states:

> At the antipodes of the monarchical principle, in theory, stands democracy, denying the right of one over others.... We know today that in the life of the nations the two theoretical principles of the ordering of the state are so elastic that they often come into reciprocal contact.... Thus the two forms of government do not exhibit an absolute antithesis, but meet at that point where the participants in power number fifty per cent.

The group of leaders balance out their views, values, and goals—not something a true Sith (devoted to the ultimate-goal fallacy) can really afford. Discussing, reflecting, and debating not only postpone reaching the inevitable goal of Sithian conquest. They might actually stop it from being reached. When we add an emotional, vulgarized version of Nietzsche's will to power into the mix, the picture becomes clear: move the questioning fools out of the way as soon as possible and as efficiently as possible. Once we open the door to having many points of view, the central goal is shaken. The Sith quest for complete power would be severely weakened because countless discussions would start fights within the movement. The discussions could make the Sith stronger intellectually, but that is not the point of Sith. The Sith tradition is about the will to power, not thinking. The point is to create one monopolistic project controlling the everyday lives of all the peoples in the galaxy. No one in the Sithian sect cared or should have cared about any values above that. If one had, he would have stopped being a full-blown Sith and started to become something else.

The story may all sound a bit unrealistic, yet we do have a perfect historical demonstration of it: Soviet Russia. Leon Trotsky, a revolutionary politician, expressed the view clearly. Read the following with "Sith" in mind where Trotsky speaks of the Communist Party:

> We can only be right with and by the Party, for history has provided no other way of being in the right. The English have a saying 'My country, right or wrong,' whether it is in the right or in the wrong, it is my country. We have much better historical justification in saying whether it is right or wrong in certain individual concrete cases, it is my party.... And if the Party adopts a decision which one or other of us thinks unjust, he will say, just or unjust, it is my Party, and I shall support the consequences of the decision to the end.

This quote represents Trotsky's views on monopolistic decision making under communist/socialist regimes. All people have to comply because otherwise, with differences of opinion, the monopolistic plan would collapse fast. There is always a problem with determining and deciding what the objective and absolute truth is—at least, so they say in the Western world. Oh silly Westerners, haven't they heard about the simple Soviet solution? The party is always right, so it becomes a perfect barometer for rightness. If you agree with the party, welcome to the party. If you disagree with the party, party time is over, gulag time is here. If the party disagrees with you, you'd better run. Trotsky eventually had to run because Stalin declared him a public enemy who had to be eliminated. Trotsky did not comply and dared to disagree. After a couple of unsuccessful attempts on his life, Stalin's secret service finally killed him in the name of unity, in the name of one project that couldn't be contested by anyone. Stalin was obsessed with a homogenous vision of Russia, but he did not simply kill his enemies. He had to prosecute them in front of the public, where they had to confess. If they did not, torture and threats to kill their families worked to convince them to declare how they had conspired to kill the utopian communist project.

It is no surprise that the Sith were in favor of abolishing the separation of powers. The modern legal system relies on the idea of the separation of powers between legislative, executive, and judicial functions. I know what you're thinking: "Do we really have three powers or only one?" To tell you the truth, in all this excitement I kind of lost track myself. Yet, surely there are some checks and balances, however imperfect, and they do function from time to time, such as when a president cannot tell the courts how to rule—a feature perfectly lacking under dictatorship and Sith control. Under dictatorship, the courts are simply following orders, just like bureaucrats.

The rule of two Sith also nicely explains why Palpatine chose such a weak person as Anakin for his apprentice. Many people complain about Anakin's character. They expected him to be much stronger, smarter, and more independent. Actually, Palpatine was wise to pick a disciple with all those weaknesses. A physically skilled and emotionally vulnerable person is more easily controllable and is also a smaller threat to his master. We will talk more about this in the second-to-last chapter of part two.

"THE TIME HAS COME. EXECUTE ORDER 66," OR "KEEP CALM AND READ MACHIAVELLI"

THE "Order 66" scene rightly deserves its fame. It perfectly captures the essence of a new political era finalizing the creation of Sith dictatorship. Our list of Palpatine's inspirations would not be complete without one last giant of political theory: Niccolò Machiavelli. How would he have commented on the ruthless order? Let him speak for himself: "The new ruler must determine all the injuries that he will need to inflict. He must inflict them once and for all." Why? Because a wounded animal must be killed. Otherwise it eventually comes back with a vengeance.

Machiavelli was the author of one of the most important books on political action: *The Prince*. It is a guide on how to win political battles in the long run. The instructions are clear and relevant for the present day too: If you are a firm believer in justice, truth, beauty, and peaceful cooperation, then politics is not the place for you. Rather than a place for inspired angels solving people's problems, politics paves the way for cruel guys and coldblooded folks. Politics expects you to have Frank Underwood's blood in your veins, not Jesus Christ's. Know how to conquer, not how to get along with others. Or pretend you get along with others, so you can conquer more. You have to catch them off balance. Do what must be done. Do not hesitate. Show no mercy. Only then will you be strong enough to realize your political ambitions and goals.

I could spend many pages drawing parallels between Palpatine's instructions and the theory of politics. Machiavelli offered many strategic pieces of advice for running political schemes. For example, it is always better to be feared than loved. How well does that fit into Vader's public relations? Fear is a powerful and lasting feeling motivating most people. Love may motivate too, but it does not guarantee as long-lasting an effect as fear. And of course, as we know from Yoda, fear is the founding element for drawing people to the Dark Side. Be feared and spread fear within the people you rule so you can create unconditional obedience. Furthermore, rulers themselves should also fear losing control, because otherwise they might lose some of their monopolized powers. It is not uncommon in authoritarian regimes to spread fear to the political elite of a bloodthirsty public just waiting to chop their heads off and start a revolution, as in Ceaușescu's case in Romania—a fear that in a totalitarian system is quite justified.

Fear is an overpowering weapon for not only mobilizing supporters, but destroying potential opposition. Your political allies may join you because they believe in your project or find you to be a strong leader. Yet what about the resistance? What about the other side of the ideological spectrum? The deadly strength of fear is a primary way to destroy the opposition. In the Third Reich, not all of the people were Hitler's supporters. Many, especially Catholics, did not adhere to his views (as the results from the elections in 1933 well show). Nevertheless, fear allows the rulers to silence such people. Not everyone can be Batman and turn fear to his own advantage to fight evil.

In any case, the tool of fear is part of the broader agenda of treating people as simple mechanical means to be moved around like objects. In dealing with others, rulers must have Machiavellian determination to achieve their goal. Any harm inflicted on their enemies has to either be deadly or at least wound so badly as to make the enemy incapable of revenge. Peace is never an option. Peace is only a break, a breathing space in which a ruler has to be prepared for more fighting. Machiavelli was not a complete monster in his descriptions of and advice for political rulers. That would be a vulgarized version of him just as much as in the case of Nietzsche and nihilism. Nevertheless, his advice is pretty malicious. Even worse, it relies on an objective fact: ruling is not a nice business. Rulers are no angels. They are Hobbesian monstrosities. Politics by its very nature is detached from ethical considerations. And if it's not, then the political system has various efficient mechanisms for forcing most ethical people out.

PART TWO: RISE OF THE EMPIRE

THE RECIPE FOR DICTATORSHIP

WE now understand Chancellor Palpatine's philosophical background and his ideological views on human beings and social arrangements. Now it is time to understand his modus operandi and path to becoming an emperor. How does he transform the Old Republic into the First Galactic Empire? Believe it or not, the change is not very easy. Every ruler is constrained, even when his enemies can draw on supernatural skills. The founding father of an empire may not have an easy path to achieving his goal—especially when he has a church to fight with, gifted with the same type of skills. The way to establish a dictatorship is not simply by taking someone else's place, such as a senator's. Creating a dictatorship is not merely a shift in the type of person in charge. Otherwise, all the necessary factors for dictatorship would already exist. The change has to be deeper, as power needs to be reformed, expanded, and transformed. In other words, the change has to be not only personal, but institutional, with support from the public.

Below I will spell out a couple of major factors in Palpatine's path to victory, which will bring us to the general recipe for dictatorship. I do not present this recipe so that someone can use it to become a tyrant (do not try this at home, please). Instead, I explain it so that anyone can see the warnings *Star Wars* offers. To make a long story short, the saga is here to caution everyone about how easy it can be to lose the freedoms we enjoy.

TRADE CONFLICT

LET us begin at the beginning. Every story has a beginning, as the trailer for Episode I tells us—Palpatine's master plan included. The story starts off with an economic conflict between Naboo and the Trade Federation, a conflict carefully orchestrated by Palpatine. The initial economic tension ignites further events, leading to serious social and political consequences. The opening contains one of the most established patterns for creating conflicts and wars between peoples. Well done, George Lucas.

Think about what constitutes a peaceful and stable society: voluntary and welcoming relations between individuals and groups. Those relations are natural on a very local level. You live with your family and friends. You meet the people you want to meet from your neighborhood. All sides choose what they want to do. It's never perfect and ideal, as some people are bored or irritated by others. A pity for some, but boundaries are not forever fixed and the social search for satisfying choices is possible. In any case, social conflicts are harder to create if people are free to build their own relations, because they recognize similarities between themselves. Once you start talking to someone about how disappointing the *Sherlock* TV series was, say, you find common ground with them. You recognize a human being, a member of the same species. And so people can get along if they have room to discover other people in a congenial manner. Their discussions are a form of exchange.

Trade is one such exchange, a type that occurs in the form of material goods and services. When you trade, you contact someone else, someone usually not related to you. In a local store, this may result in a chat, though this is not the case for traders living far, far away from you. Locally you may also interact with many people without engaging in economic transactions. With people far away, trade becomes more difficult, although in the era of the internet it is much easier. Nevertheless, people trade between regions, countries, and continents. By trading, people cooperate throughout the globe and create impressive things without genetic bonding. Yes, I know that directly applies to just some people. After all, by buying coffee from abroad you have no contact with Brazilians. Nevertheless, some entrepreneurs from your nation do have business with them, do cooperate with them. Hence they create some form of socioeconomic bond. Provided business is good, we have some amount of flourishing on both sides.

How does that relate to the story of Episode I? To start a war, you need to kill trade or at least seriously damage it. If people from two different regions are highly economically integrated, if lots of them are doing business together, it is very hard for rulers to create a social dynamic favoring war. Also, with huge inter-regional business connections, benign lobbies are created—lobbies against waging war. You remember *The Godfather*: wars and fights are bad for business for both sides. Only aggressive rulers that gain their positions through expansionary power benefit from war. People voluntarily cooperating and trading are simply hurt, so they oppose war.

If there is no trade, however, starting a war becomes easier. As someone once said, "If soldiers are not to cross international borders, goods must do so." To revise the quote slightly, "If soldiers are to cross international borders, goods must not do so." Indeed, the story of Europe in the twentieth century demonstrates this fact well. During the Great Depression, various governments, including the United States' (through the famous Smoot-Hawley Tariff Act), started protectionist policies to support minor business groups. By significantly increasing tariffs, world economic cooperation started to crumble, ultimately increasing the power of nationalists and national socialists and leading to hostile attitudes between nations. Those developments and additional important changes eventually led to the Second World War. What happened afterward also confirms the observation. European governments started to reach advanced economic integration. For example, the French and German economies are right now so integrated—trade and capital flows are at such high rates—that it is very hard to imagine another war between them. There is simply too much to lose from conflict. There is also too much visible good from the current state of affairs to promote nationalist sentiments among the public sufficient to ignite an open conflict.

There is more to the story though. As we know, trade between Naboo and other planets was blocked by the Trade Federation. Yet wasn't the purpose of the Trade Federation to facilitate trade and make sure exchanges ran smoothly? Why did it have armies that seemed highly attack-oriented? (You can recognize a difference between an army aiming to defend and an army aiming to attack.) Here is another echo of the real world in *Star Wars*: the trade organizations around us are not necessarily and exclusively about trade. They may actually be about politics and control. The European Union is a perfect example. On the one hand, it carries the abovementioned benefit of integrating peoples on the European continent. On the other hand, it produces tremendous amounts of bureaucracy and regulations, which are potential sources of political control. Thus the Trade Federation, run by Nute Gunray, captures the modern world of economic diplomacy perfectly: As a country, you may not be allowed to trade freely in goods and services. You may have to ask for a permission to do so—because the federation is there to decide.

Debates about sophisticated trade agreements such as NAFTA, CETA, EFTA, the EU, and so forth concern precisely this problem. Are they angels bringing trade and cooperation, or are they demons burdening societies with regulation? Without answering definitively, one thing may be obvious: trade agreements have the potential for corruption. And they allow the federations' powers to grow. Palpatine needed the Trade Federation to enact an effective blockade. Now imagine there was no Trade Federation licensing trade and trade was free, with Naboo inviting any interested business partners. The apparently legal blockade would not have been possible because there would have been no official body to make a decision. Of course, technically the blockade could still have happened, but for any outside observer it would have been blatantly obvious that it constituted aggression. Imagine that some of Palpatine's agents showed up and blocked the routes for galactic commerce. The Republic would have immediately recognized them as intruders: *Who gave you the right to do what you do? Get your spaceships away from their routes right now.*

Yet in the case of the Trade Federation, which is recognized by the Republic and has the prerogative to block trade, it is not immediately obvious that the Republic should see things this way. The federation has some accepted and established rights to intervene. As someone says, "Who knows whether it is justified? We have to create a commission to study the case."

To summarize, Palpatine wanted to create a conflict between two sides to encourage one of them to cry out for more power to be given to the chancellor. There is no better way to create a conflict than to destroy or seriously burden trade. Hostility increases, wealth decreases. People develop negative emotions and become ready to act decisively to take revenge. War may become an option. Plus, if trade is already burdened, then the cost of war drops down a bit. If we are already not trading, then starting a war will not cause a loss in trading.

In general, any expanding imperial state likes to feed itself by presenting itself as necessary to fight an economic crisis. A crisis in trade is just one of those instances. It is an empirical tendency of human history that dictatorship arises often in severe economic downturns.

Democracy as Bureaucracy

GET ready for the big news, news that makes you realize that *Star Wars* is cleverer than you thought: Palpatine did not design everything. Not every bad thing in the saga resulted from a well-designed plan. Surely a lot of conspiring had to be done, but it happened within a specific political system with obvious deficiencies. The trade conflict was a good starting point for creating a socioeconomic crisis, in turn triggering the chain of events that led to the rise of the Empire. Nevertheless, the results were far from obvious, initially. Conflicts can be resolved, and problems may be solved. Galactic democracy, however, suffers from eternal flaws, as we can see in Episode I—flaws instantly recognizable in the bureaucracies of our modern political systems.

I am sure you remember Palpatine whispering to Queen Amidala during the discussion of the trade conflict that started the whole course of events in motion: "The chancellor has little real power. He is mired by baseless accusations of corruption. The bureaucrats are in charge now." Such skepticism of the government is well-founded, since central governments do not solve local problems. They play games with lobbies and other interest groups, so that the government policy is always a result of myriad connections across the country. How true that becomes when we talk about the *galaxy*! You have a problem? Then report it to some bureau and wait.

We have governmental rules, decisions, interpretations, investigations, meetings, consultations even in the simplest of matters. They are not really the result of vindictive decisions by democratic governments. This is just how governments function: through basing their rules on arbitrarily chosen numbers. They do not really have other ways to form their rules, as they are totally different from private companies. Companies rely on two strong forces: consumers buying their products, and investors financing them. The investors themselves are usually interested in finding consumers, as the money they invest has to be recouped from revenues of some kind. The mechanism for adjustment and control is very easy: Once you make your clients angry, you're out. Once you make investors angry, they can say goodbye even before you get the chance to mess things up.

Obviously, by the very nature of bureaucracy in a democratic government, such market-based methods simply cannot be employed. Voting every four years in no way changes the essence of the government. As implied by the word "government," it governs, gives instructions, and imposes some order onto society. It does not rely on consumers' decisions the way companies usually do. Of course, governments are composed of and built by people, some of whom have genuinely good intentions. Those people honestly try to create rules and conduct themselves in a way that can help make their governments better. Yet this is problematic: big centralized institutions are doing lots of things at the same time without being constrained by consumer choice in any real way. Therefore they will always have problems in trying to create a good standard for assessing their decisions. The result is that they come up with some numbers that serve to measure how well they are realizing their stated goals. The officials and bodies state their targets and a year later see how well they have done. And so develops an obsession with formal procedures, which are meant to function as a standard—which of course they cannot do. By their nature, they are arbitrary, which in turn changes the possibilities for action within government. The literature on collective decision making shows bureaucracy's troublesome nature.

The political theorist Anthony Downs demonstrated why bureaus have to be hierarchical and how information flows through them in such a way that no one knows fully what is going on in the organization. Bureaus are constructed by their political sponsors in such a way that all relevant interests can be taken into account. The hierarchical structure of bureaus inevitably leads to lags in transmitting information and taking action based on it.

That is why even when faced with the simplest of all possible cases, an illegal blockade, the chancellor hesitates to make a decision. Amidala is furious, and rightly so. Palpatine takes the occasion to repeat once more, "Enter the bureaucrats—the true rulers of the Republic." He was telling the truth, though only to help achieve his own goals. Before settling the case, the chancellor wanted to have an independent commission investigate the blockade and ongoing conflict. But hadn't that just happened when the Jedi were sent to Naboo and went through the blockade? Wasn't it enough that they saw the invasion with their own eyes? Apparently not. But that is not a flaw in the movie, as some critics think. It is rather another perfect demonstration of how Jar Jar Binks-ish government bodies can be.

After abstaining from banishing the blockaders, the chancellor advised the government to start the whole process of bureaucratic settlement, in which the Trade Federation (and its lobbyists) would have a say. In the meantime, killing off trade with Naboo resulted in a major humanitarian crisis (in which not only humans suffered). No wonder Amidala fell for Palpatine's advice immediately: *Get rid of this Chancellor Valorum right away. Let us vote for non-confidence now. We need new, strong leadership to do something right away.*

Dictators rise to power in this way. They spot obvious problems with democratic orders and their awful bureaus and offer a panacea: *Elect me, and I will take care of everything. I promise to solve all the troubling issues, resolve conflicts, get rid of poverty, and of course get rid of the nasty bureaucracy. If anything goes wrong, I will simple say it should not go wrong. Problem solved.* We've heard this so many times, especially during campaigns. Welcome to the world of politics. Cheers to Episode I for capturing it. Episode IV then shows the evolution from parliamentary government to dictatorship. What remained of parliament was dissolved, and the regional officials of the Emperor governed directly.

Yet Palpatine's recipe for getting rid of bureaucracy by direct rule is a demagogic and cheap trick. As Anthony Downs insightfully commented:

> Eliminating waste from bureaus is ... absurd because no human organization ever devotes anywhere near 100 per cent of its efforts to achieving its formal purposes directly. Hence a certain amount of "waste" is inevitable.... These conclusions do not mean that every bureau is perfect and all present behavior is necessary. However, they imply that distinguishing "waste" from "non-waste" is much more difficult and involves far greater subtleties than is usually admitted by the critics of bureaucracy.

In other words, if you buy into the whole idea of advanced political prerogatives, be prepared to face bureaucracy, because it is inevitable. In imposing his rule onto the galaxy, Palpatine has to create his own local bureaucracies, which are even more inefficient than those under the Old Republic. The only way to avoid bureaucracy is to rely on forces outside of politics.

Palpatine tricks one of the most honest politicians in the series, Amidala. She understands the political process perfectly. She is not fascinated with power. She believes in her ideals, but more importantly, she sees the dangers of centralized power and expanding governmental bodies. She recognizes the psychology behind the people's support for the government. Too bad she did not recognize the power grab soon enough (admittedly, she is also not good at choosing boyfriends). The tragedy of political systems is precisely that they push even good people into making wrong choices by using the concept of "the lesser evil." A lesser evil is still an evil, even if it's committed by good people. A potential dictator creates situations in which "less evil" choices will take us closer and closer to an evil system. After all, lesser evil is a step toward evil, only a smaller one.

SOCIETY NEEDS AN ENEMY

HERE we reach the darkest of the dark aspects of the human species: how is it that people come to support dictators? How is it even possible that Palpatine would be elected and stay in power? Of course, fear plays a role, but first you have to empower the man and make sure he stays in power. What is the motivation for the initial support for political monsters? Surely it has to involve having a public that lacks imagination and knowledge. But that is not sufficient. Why then do people support the monsters? Apparently because they have someone whom they despise even more. In other words, they have an enemy that has to be fought with passion and determination. Release your social anger!

You can feel it. It makes society stronger, gives it focus. People are collective animals, and species in *Star Wars* demonstrate this feature. Like us, they live in herds, which creates space for the individual to relate his or her identity to some group or class. Unfortunately, at the same time this feature leads people to aggressively separate their group from other groups and suggest that everything awful about the world comes from those other groups. It comes from the Others.

You probably know the TV series *Lost*, which capitalizes on the idea that organizing society and devising social rules is so much easier when you can threaten them with "Others" standing ready to chop your head off and steal your food and children. This idea stems from the political thought of the famous German philosopher Carl Schmitt (you guessed it: he lived in the 1930s). His words strongly express that having a social enemy is a powerful aid for directing the masses: "As long as the state is a political entity this requirement for internal peace compels it in critical situations to decide also upon the domestic enemy. Every state provides, therefore, some kind of formula for the declaration of an internal enemy."

The purpose of politics is to think about the enemies to be fought with passion and vengeance—to be absolutely determined, almost like Agent Smith from *The Matrix*. It is purpose that created us. Purpose that connects us. Purpose that pulls us. That guides us. That drives us. It is purpose that defines us. Purpose that binds us. Do you think you haven't been caught up in social anger? Are you sure? As a species, we even learn to use words that ignite emotional reactions. That is how we evolved. That is why there is still hateful collectivism in the world: we automatically tend to see representatives of the Others as a threat to our resources and culture. That is why many people listen to "Waiting for the Worms," by Pink Floyd: while listening to it, under their skin they feel how hateful propaganda can appeal to virtually anyone.

Politics is about conflicts—not solving existing conflicts, but inciting new ones. *Star Wars* perfectly captures this idea too. We often fall prey to a utopian vision in which governments create social harmony. But that doesn't happen, because social anger drives people to support politicians. Someone has to be stopped, someone has to be taxed, someone has to be regulated, something has to be outlawed. The whole idea of "lesser evils" is a perfect demonstration of how unattractive politics is: You are against someone, and you derive tremendous energy from your opposition, driving you into politics. During political debates, you have to crush an opponent, not chat with him in a friendly environment. That calls to mind one of the paradoxes of social media: even though it has magnificent potential to unite people from all different backgrounds, it also allows them to create separate-group utopias, in which outsiders are seen as enemies (hence the reason why politics has become so radicalized since the advent of the internet).

What are the features of social enemies that influence the political atmosphere? Do they have to be like orcs in *Lord of the Rings*? Herr Schmitt goes on:

The political enemy need not be morally evil or aesthetically ugly; he need not appear as an economic competitor, and it may even be advantageous to engage with him in business transactions. But he is, nevertheless, the other, the stranger; and it is sufficient for his nature that he is, in a specially intense way, existentially something different and alien, so that in the extreme case conflicts with him are possible. These can neither be decided by a previously determined general norm nor by the judgment of a disinterested and therefore neutral third party.

As we know from dozens of historical experiences, the simplest ways to differentiate people and create primitive reactions and conflicts are through characteristics such as race, nationality, and language that the masses recognize almost straightaway.

Even though race, nationality, and language are the most common, the differences may be subtler. The enemy may come from another group, as was the case of property owners in Russia during the Soviet revolution. Someone has to be one of the Others, another tribe, so that it should be possible to put the blame on them for society's problems. I use the word "tribe" since it is related to our deep biological instincts.

How does it all fit into the *Star Wars* story? Who is the enemy Palpatine has to fight? The separatists, of course. They are different: they do not want to submit; they do not want to join our team. Hence we will show them what to do: we will make them love us, or we will crush them. One might argue that *Star Wars* is unrealistic because it fails to depict racism even with all the racial diversity we see. Yet it presents perfectly something dark about human nature—a sin more fundamental than racism: people's readiness to hunt and destroy others simply because they are part of some other group. Racism, fascism, communism, and other evils are all results of that initial sin.

Palpatine is capable of mobilizing societies to stand with him because he is skillful enough to convince the people of the "ugliness" of the separatists. The irrational emotions of the peoples of the Republic are so off base that they do not hesitate to empower the monster with deadly weapons and armies to create a disastrous conflict and tyrannical society. The peoples are ready to empower him because he is a weapon against the Others—and surely he is not going to threaten them, right?

DEMOCRACY NEEDS ITS FOOLS

EMPOWERING the monster certainly requires at least a little bit of stupidity. In other words, every dictator has a Jar Jar Binks in the background. Obviously Jar Jar's character was created for comic relief. Yet with all his obvious shortcomings, mindless lines, bizarre behavior, and unintentionally unfunny moments, the main achievement of having such a character in the story was actually excellent. Jar Jar was morally responsible for significantly empowering Palpatine through his proposal to create the Grand Army of the Republic—a necessary means for the creation of a tyrannical Sithian state.

Palpatine had to rise to power through legal means: the remainders of a democratic process. Someone had to propose creating a new army that would allow the creation of a dangerous state. Of course, Jar Jar offered his help to the chancellor in need. The road to hell is paved with good intentions, and so was Jar Jar's head filled with them. We can only regret that the creators of the *Star Wars* were not successful in making him more likeable. Imagine if Jar Jar was more like C-3PO from the original trilogy. Imagine if we grew to actually cherish Jar Jar and enjoy his company. How much more powerful would that make it when he became the proponent of emergency powers for the chancellor? And how much more realistic?

One of the most noticeable aspects of *Star Wars'* evolution is how the series' portrayal of good versus evil gets more realistic. We start off with the shallowest possible portrayal in *A New Hope,* in which good and evil are almost completely separated (with perhaps a few people hesitating to make a choice). With *The Empire Strikes Back* and *Return of the Jedi,* the portrayal goes deeper. The prequel trilogy goes even further and finally breaks away from simplistic moral divisions. In the original trilogy, one can be good by simply following good emotions and having balanced instincts. Making a bad decision is virtually always conscious. *You know well you are doing a bad thing. You chose the Dark Side knowingly.*

In the prequel trilogy, many characters are simply ignorant and make bad choices that result in worse consequences even though they are not at all on the Dark Side. The case of military powers and Jar Jar is a great example. That poor, nice CGI rabbit—who could blame him? He wanted to do something good. Let us be honest, however. He should never ever be in such a position. Empowering the fool with such a prerogative was the quickest way to make something crazy happen. If the political and legal system rests on this type of mind, then it is simply suicidal. As economist Bryan Caplan (author of *The Myth of the Rational Voter: Why Democracies Choose Bad Policies*) noted: "Good intentions are ubiquitous in politics; what is scarce is accurate beliefs."

The initial trilogy taught us that to achieve its goals, the Dark Side can either bribe you with benefits or blackmail you. The prequels tell us more. The Dark Side can simply fool people. Ignorance is a powerful weapon to manipulate the people. Palpatine is quite well fitted for the role of a grand manipulator. Most of the prequels' story is based on how ignorance can be exploited with unwitting help by good people. Unfortunately, all those good people paid a price for their lack of vision.

Democratic systems are based on oligarchical rule. In parliaments and congresses, we do not have independent thinkers. We have parties, and parties are collective entities within which we have a few leaders. People are eager to follow them. Likewise with the many members of legislative bodies who are ready to blindly accept someone else's leadership—even if that someone else is promoting evil solutions. After all, for any evil, one can easily find a greater evil to ease the conscience.

The fundamental element of democracy is that political groups—as with any groups—follow the leader most of the time without questioning. This guarantees that, masochistically, they will even vote to destroy their own society. We are happy because we supported and favored our political leader.

One of the smartest lines in the whole series is Amidala's depressing comment about how "liberty dies with thunderous applause." Marketing of ill policies can be very impressive. People clap when their liberties are taken away because they are drugged by inadequately understood emotions and visions. Once, in Poland, the government wanted to impose a new tax on large supermarket chains. Many people cheered it even though they would directly suffer from the new fiscal burden because it would weaken competition and cause higher prices. Why did they cheer? Because the government marketed the policy as levying a tax on sneaky, greedy foreign corporations. *We will show them our power!*

This kind of trick is often performed by governments. Just like that, the Republic suddenly changed into a superstate. A dangerous tyranny was created by delegating special powers to the chancellor, but who cares? *We will show those dirty separatists who's da boss!* Tempting indeed. This is how all propaganda works: it clouds rational judgment with emotions. While the mind malfunctions, nightmares become reality.

Amidala, certainly one of the smartest people in the series, should hate Jar Jar's position. It does not make much sense for her to sympathize with him, as she should have been the one telling him to step down. Admittedly, he helped to create peace with the Gungans, but his role should have ended there. Winston Churchill once said that "the best argument against democracy is a five-minute conversation with Jar Jar Binks." Okay, I've slightly misquoted him. He spoke of the "average voter." He was quite wrong. The bigger problem than the average voter's ignorance is the ignorance of the people in power, who are equipped with various political tools to exploit the situation to their own benefit or the benefit of their friends.

As many readers know, George Lucas, while preparing the prequels' scripts, was inspired in part by the story of Hitler's rise to power. The term "emergency powers" actually refers directly to the circumstances in Germany when Hitler receive special powers because of the apparent threat of a communist revolution (though historians suspect his thugs burned the German parliament and blamed the communists). The so-called Enabling Act virtually abolished parliament and the constitution too. The act was supported by the majority of the parliament and signed by the German president, Paul von Hindenburg. The politicians were acting very much like Jar Jar Binks, despite being people you would not have expected to be at his intellectual level.

Democracy has its fools. And they are indispensable on the path to tyranny. But *Star Wars* did not have enough screen time to show that political foolishness is a vice not to be associated only with mindless characters like Jar Jar. In reality, it often characterizes otherwise-smart people.

DESTRUCTION OF THE OPPOSITION, AND THE BALANCE OF POWER

THE great dictator has to be the great monopolist, the one and only. No other leader can share his powers in any field—especially in terms of controlling other people's behavior. To achieve a full monopoly, one has to take over the tools of the state, especially the ones that allow for "special powers." During this process, any potential political rivals must be destroyed. This concerns both competing centers of power and ideological alternatives. In *Star Wars*, both of those are embodied in the Jedi, the chancellor's strongest enemies. The Jedi are both a religious organization influencing people's behavior and a formal power in the state apparatus as it has obvious prerogatives.

As public officials, the Jedi are allowed to intervene as ambassadors, interrogators, police, and detectives. They are also a kind of secret service working closely with the Senate. At least, this is what we learn in Episode III. Additionally, the Jedi are almost like a state within the state. Nobody elects them. Nobody appoints them. Nobody performs any sensible audit of what they do. They have their own council, which sets its own rules. They are possibly one of the most significant powers in the galaxy. Up until the creation of the Grand Army of the Republic and the delegation of special powers, the chancellor had a relatively weak position dominated by the bureaucrats. Compared to the Jedi, his powers were almost negligible. The Jedi are like a central bank or supreme court, an agency not subject to the normal electoral process but consisting of an elite ruling themselves. It is very hard to dismiss them.

Naturally, such an independent body has to be taken down as it threatens the dictator's project. Of course, I do not mean to imply such bodies are perfect or necessary for society to function well. In the real world, they can actually be obstacles to proper change. On the other hand, they are often a great weapon for at least slowing down some radical politicians and their appetites for control. In political science, there is an expression for these weapons: checks and balances, which can effectively put brakes on a lot of decisions, both good and bad. They can surely put the brake on the creation of power centralized in one place, which is always associated with the totalitarian idea.

Independent institutions must come under attack in order for the chancellor to evolve into the Emperor, and it may be very easy to do so from the populist perspective. We do not see public rage against the Jedi, but the chancellor could easily pull off effective propaganda against them. *Look at those buffoons in their brown robes, so sure of themselves, so vain and presumptuous, never listening, never really caring about the people and their needs, only sitting in their comfy armchairs telling you to chill when you show up with a real problem. And we have no control over them. This has to be stopped. The democratic process has to govern everyone, even the Jedi, who, it turns out, want to seize power through an attempt on the chancellor's life. Now they want to put themselves in the position of ultimate rulers, not only as policemen, but prosecutors and judges too.* (Remember Mace Windu's words: "He is too dangerous to be kept alive.")

A totalitarian government faces potential opposition from three areas: formal powers, political rivals aspiring to take over those powers, and the sphere of ideas. Competing or unconvinced politicians can be killed or arrested (like they were after the vote for special powers given to Hitler). The Jedi are attacked as a competing power within the government, but also as a rival ideological force. They have a different worldview, and they may inspire people or encourage them to think about other values. Remember that when the totalitarian state finally arrives, fear is a crucial element in sustaining it and stopping people from revolting. Here we have a philosophy that suggests the people get rid of any fears and take a stand against the tyrant. This threatens the expansionary state because in the end it does not have much to offer besides blackmail.

Real-world historical cases of oppressive states confirm this strategy. Stalin and his army of ruthless killers did everything to destroy any possible human institution influencing people's lives: societies, bonds, religion, marriage, family. People's motivations leading them to action are grounded in such surroundings. The oppressive state does everything to extinguish these institutions as fast as possible so that the only thing remaining is the totalitarian god. If you've read George Orwell's *1984* (and I hope you have), you know the totalitarian apparatus's obsession with making people love Big Brother. This was not something Orwell invented, as Stalin actually tried to implement the lie that everyone loved Soviet Russia. All of the supposed traitors to his state were made by torture and threats to publicly admit they were not worthy of Soviet trust and hence had to be eliminated from society. That was just a farce, of course, but one that made it seem as if the only way to find peace and harmony was through loyalty to a dreadful murderer parading as a savior.

Back to the main point: Palpatine has to issue Order 66 to build his dictatorship because it could not develop alongside a competing power centers in the government or in society generally. People respect the Jedi as peaceful monks, and offer them shelter and food while they travel. They are seen as good negotiators ready to help in crisis situations. Teaching about the Force apparently has a wide range of public support. As they would never be dragged into Palpatine's plan and convinced to join the Dark Side, the Jedi have to be taken care of with brute force. *Either you're with me, or you're my enemy.*

There is another lesson to be learned from the chancellor's strategy. To make the opposition significantly weaker, one can make it rot from the inside. Hence, the move to make Anakin the government's main agent on the council—simple and brilliant. Remember *The Godfather*'s greatest management quote? "Keep your friends close, but your enemies closer." Why? Not only to know what they're doing, but also to exert at least some influence on their actions. Even if Anakin does not eventually choose the Dark Side and does not become the next Sith, his contribution to upsetting the council from within will be substantial.

CREATION OF THE NEW SECRET SERVICE

Now we get to the darkest of the dark corners of political systems: secret services. Talking about them is always tricky. Why do they invite so much controversy?

The reason is very simple: secret services are beyond direct legal control, while other social institutions, both private and public, are monitored on many levels. The secret-service thread in *Star Wars* is not much developed, but at a certain point we learn its importance. Yes, you guessed it: Order 66 again. Out of nowhere, we learn about the loyal army of soldiers receiving very secret instructions directly from the chancellor himself to kill off every single enemy of the Republic—every Jedi.

Notice the obvious conspiracy behind this. The chancellor in previous circumstances was not very strong. He was surrounded by raging bureaucrats who indirectly controlled him. As in democracy, specific procedures, carefully designed rules, govern how the official should act. The point applies to all public officials whose behavior can be monitored by other individuals within the government and who in turn can be controlled, questioned, and assessed in carrying out their responsibilities. Not everyone can be subject only to the chancellor. It works only if the group is small enough, and also directly working under the command of the chancellor and beyond any other control and surveillance. Welcome to the secret service under Order 66.

A typical prime minister under typical democratic procedures cannot really lead a perfect conspiracy. It is just too difficult to pull off since there are formal relations and rules that make it visible to some. And that "some" means dozens or even more bureaucrats, so you cannot keep the conspiracy a secret. Therefore it has to take place outside of democratic procedures so that it should be much, much easier to not tell many people. Under the modern democratic system, this is possible through measures of national security—interpreted of course in a very broad manner. In other words, there are ways to get away with some forms of conspiracy, to make various decisions confidently and unseen by the public. The secret may come out, but sometimes it can take a long time, as with the 1953 Iranian coup d'état orchestrated by the Central Intelligence Agency, which the CIA admitted only sixty years later.

Don't get me wrong: I am not presenting the nutty case that everything is organized and orchestrated by secret agencies. Not at all. Nevertheless, they can have a quite powerful influence on our lives. Since they are a significant part of the government, and have secret yet powerful ways to affect the political sphere, the dictator has to replace them with his own people or dissolve the existing secret services and start new ones. The latter precisely describes Order 66, under which Palpatine conspired behind everyone else's backs to create a new secret agency directly responsible to him. And Order 66 dissolved a previous sort of secret police, the Jedi, who would never have become loyal to the Emperor, for obvious reasons.

Aside from revolutionary times, such agencies are not built completely from scratch. They take over the existing government architecture to pave the way for an awful regime. Consider Germany again. The Reichstag was set on fire, supposedly by a communist. To protect German civilization, the public and many politicians were convinced to give special powers to the chancellor. Was it a false flag? Was the fire actually set by the secret agents of Hitler? The conspiracy version of the story is tempting, as the whole picture of political revolution becomes complete. Unfortunately we do not have definitive evidence, although it's hard to believe that the one communist that got caught organized and executed everything himself.

Bearing in mind Hitler's possible conspiracy to start the fire in the Reichstag, Lucas presented an alluring possibility: Palpatine kidnapped himself. It was not really the separatists. Just as Jeffrey Lebowski said, find the one who benefits. (Or wait, was it John Lennon?) Palpatine created a political crisis—a trade conflict and a separatist conflict—and then kidnapped himself with the help of Count Dooku. The need to abolish freedom became more compelling.

And none of this would have happened had it not been for the Order 66 secret service. It does not explain the whole story, as we know from the above. Nevertheless, without the conspiracy, Palpatine would not have succeeded.

FOLLOWERS MUST BE INTELLECTUALLY WEAK

LET me guess: you were disappointed with the Anakin Skywalker we got to know in the first three episodes. Guess what? The Emperor does not share your disappointment and finds your lack of appreciation disturbing.

You remember the discussion above about the oligarchical nature of evolving groups. Oligarchy is sort of egalitarianism within the upper group. If the group is larger in numbers, then the quest for monopoly is threatened. The smart Sithian solution is the rule of two in order to make sure a larger number of Sith doesn't cause internal fights between Sith allies. There remains a critical difficulty, however: there can still be a fight between a master and an apprentice.

Who knows this better than Palpatine himself? As we learn from Episode III, he was educated by his master, Darth Plagueis the Dupe—I mean, the Wise. Palpatine was a very intelligent student of the Dark Side. He was skilled, and finally realized it was time to take over from the master. Plagueis could be taken care of and removed from the scene. Palpatine was patient, confident, clever, and gifted with foresight, a completely all-around player (also good with animals). One can hardly find his deficiencies, as he was good at practicing the Dark Side. His master plan worked out smoothly, and he definitely won initially.

Knowing his own story of having taken over from the master, he again demonstrated cleverness. Palpatine could not have a Palpatine type as his student, because the master would eventually end up like Plagueis. When you plan to monopolize control, dominate the universe, and introduce your own unlimited power, you cannot afford to create a follower potentially stronger than you. That person should be noticeably, significantly weaker—so as to pose no serious threat.

Only now, at the end, do you understand: Anakin was actually filling a specific role in the first three episodes. You're welcome. Palpatine needed a whining, weak boy who was not very smart and didn't have a great philosophical understanding of the Force. The boy needed to possess great physical skills and a ruthless character to enable him to direct a tyrannical army and introduce universal terror to the people. He needed to lack strong morals but be keen to act on emotion, just as the Dark Side recommends. He also had to be easily manipulated, ready to give way to virtually anyone who gives him enough attention. Such a vulnerable man requires only praise and a pat on the back to convince him to be obedient. An orphan who had no good father figure and who had been taken away from his mother at a very early age must have sounded like a promising investment. He would be weak enough to manipulate: give him shortcuts to pleasure and satisfaction, and he would be ready to follow the path.

That partly explains the shallowness of the opera scene in Episode III. Palpatine seems to be almost bored by the trivial one-liners Anakin has learned from the Jedi's propaganda office. "The greater good" seems like a catchphrase functioning as an answer to almost anything. If you like to point to the strong deficiencies of the prequel trilogy, I know it may ruin your mood, but this is how things are. Some of you are inclined to say to the director: "I know it was you, George. You broke my heart." But, sorry, it was not him. It was Palpatine, who perfectly knew what he wanted to achieve. Anakin is molded for the job of Palpatine's apprentice. I know you expected more from Darth Vader: you wanted him to be Bruce Wayne or Tony Stark. He should have been nothing of the sort. The apprentice had to be like Anakin to fit the role of a mindless chief of the Nazi-like enforcement program. Stalin had his ruthless Nikolai Yezhov, the chief of secret Soviet policy responsible for raining terror on Russia (he earned the nickname "Bloody Dwarf"). Anakin was to serve a similar role: running the oppressive apparatus and making sure every single enemy of the Republic was hunted down and terminated. His job was not to become a teacher, mentor, or philosopher. If you think tyrannical minds are to be intellectually strong and reflecting, then you should have more understanding of how dictatorship functions.

Here also lies another brilliant aspect of *Star Wars* and its depiction of who gets to the top of the ladder in in a powerful state. During the Second World War, a great Austrian thinker, Friedrich von Hayek, who wrote an illuminating book called *The Road to Serfdom*. The book offers a thorough account of how totalitarian regimes come about by reshaping social and political rules. In a way, the book amounts to a compelling story of what happened in the prequel trilogy. One chapter explains Darth Vader's rise to the head of the totalitarian regime. Okay, the book is from 1944, so the title is "Why the Worst Get on Top." But here is a nice quote applicable to Anakin:

> To be a useful assistant in the running of a totalitarian state it is not enough that a man should be prepared to accept specious justification of vile deeds, he must himself be prepared actively to break every moral rule he has ever known if this seems necessary to achieve the end set for him. Since it is the supreme leader who alone determines the ends, his instruments must have no moral convictions of their own. They must, above all, be unreservedly committed to the person of the leader; but next to this the most important thing is that they should be completely unprincipled and literally capable of everything. They must have no ideals of their own which they want to realise, no ideas about right or wrong which might interfere with the intentions of the leader.

Hence we have a reason why Palpatine made Anakin his chief follower: Anakin was not very wise. His dialogue with Amidala in Episode II shows his shallow understanding of the political process. His arguments in that exchange are so undeveloped and naïve that one can only wonder what on earth Amidala sees in him besides his physical attractiveness. I know, you were also unimpressed by his arguments and were inclined to think: "The script is weak." But in fact it is not. It captures the simplistic and superficial thinking of Anakin. Yes, defenders of nightmarish systems can be much more sophisticated and much smarter, but according to Palpatine's plan, Anakin was not to be one of them. If you think Anakin should not have been a candidate for chief follower, then you should question Palpatine's abilities. I am sure you do not want to do that.

Totalitarian regimes—including in *Star Wars*—are uniform in various aspects. Art gets destroyed. Architecture becomes primitive and loses any cheerful accents. The regime expects the people not to question the official line of thinking. Everyone has to participate in a big farce. Hollowness penetrates all aspects of human life as the quest for governmental centralization achieves full force. Intellectual life is no different. The second-most important person in the galaxy is a sad man who can only impress us with his ruthlessness. This all amounts to a carefully designed, icy, totalitarian world.

CONTROL THE DANGERS

EVERY political and social system has a tendency to arrive at an equilibrium that keeps it in place. At the same time, every system is threatened by the possibility of revolution or outright collapse—a feature certainly true of very oppressive systems, which quickly lose popular support. Therefore to avoid downfall, a dictatorship must take precautionary steps. As we know, Palpatine is a careful planner. He is perfectly aware of the danger, and so he creates necessary checks to keep everything in its place.

How do you control the dangers? In the same way as when installing the dictatorship: make sure people make the "right" decisions, "right" meaning that people choose paths that do not undermine Palpatinedom. You can convince people to do what you want them to do, in the quickest possible way: by fear. Fear is a powerful and fundamental weapon for directing people to do immoral things. It is also a vital tool to simply stop people from opposing the oppressive ruler, and make them tolerate the regime. Yet you cannot rule by fear alone.

In the original *Star Wars* trilogy, we usually see the military side of the Empire: the relationship between Vader—as commander—and his subordinates. At times we get a glimpse of the civilians who are uninterested in rebellion. They do not like the Empire, but they also don't openly oppose it: their criticism is somewhat muted. These are obvious signs of social fear firmly established. But we get most of the proof of fear by looking at relations within the army.

In several scenes, Darth Vader shows his psychopathic tendencies and threatens or simply kills his subordinates because they failed to accomplish some task. After seeing a few examples, one can hardly avoid asking: who would ever want to take on a job as a subordinate like that?

Except for some masochistic people or extreme risk lovers, hardly anyone would. It would also be very hard to organize an army from such people though. There are three possible reasons why you would want to work under Vader and accept his commands. First, the military could pay you lots of money. Second, it could pay you moderately, but the alternative is completely miserable. If you choose not to take the job, then you or your family may starve. So in a way they pay you lots of money, but only relatively. Or third, you take the job with a blaster aimed at your head. You get an offer that you can't refuse.

The reality may be a combination of the three, of course. In the first three movies, we don't get a definite answer to the question of what motivates people to work with the Empire. It may depend on the planet. We get more information in *Rogue One: A Star Wars Story*: Some people are simply ordered to cooperate. If they decline, they suffer tremendously. Blackmail and the spread of fear are the lifeblood of a highly functioning dictatorship. Do as they say, or else.

Fear is also something that cascades easily in a totalitarian regime. No other emotion can be transmitted through society with such horrifying results (a sad reason that also explains the efficiency of terrorism). As psychologist Jordan Peterson notes, under totalitarian regimes the tyrant becomes present up and down the social ladder. Because anyone can report you as a public enemy, and every other person knows you may report him, it becomes natural to participate in the big lie built around the "great" leader. The military structure is perfect example, but we have good reasons to assume it worked similarly for all societies in *Star Wars*—or at least where imperial troops are present and determined to maintain a Sithian order.

If you ever wondered why people would support Palpatine, you can also ask yourself why people would support Stalin and accept his rule. Simple: the alternative was to be tortured, hanged, and given promises of the same for your family.

So Yoda was right, and Batman in echoing Yoda was right too: fear is a major requirement for making people helpless against evil. But while this works for most, it doesn't necessarily work for everyone, as some courageous people—some Batmans and Yodas—are out there. Though not large in number, they have hearts big enough to keep them fearless, determined to change things, and strong enough to challenge the tyrant's unlimited power. As a tyrant, how do you handle the people who believe the only thing to fear is fear itself?

You have two ways to contain such threats. The first is to buy out the resistors. You simply offer the biggest rewards possible. The second option is to present them with a "lesser evil" (a favorite trick of the Joker when plotting against Batman and the people of Gotham). If you have seen the greatest TV show of all time—*The Wire*—you know you indeed have two ways to convince people to do things without using physical force: Corrupt their hearts or their minds. Corrupting their hearts simply means getting them to stop believing they are doing something evil. Corrupting their minds means allowing them to know they're doing evil, but get them to rationalize it to themselves as necessary. Two politicians from *The Wire* are good demonstrations. Senator Davis is simply corrupt at heart. Mayor Carcetti, on the other hand, has a corrupt way of thinking: *I have to do these crazy things because otherwise they'll kick me out of office, and then I'd be deprived of power to do good, right?*

The obvious danger to Palpatinedom in the original trilogy is Luke Skywalker. You cannot force him to do things. He has the courage and the skills to resist. So how do you convince him to act how you want? You create circumstances that push him toward an evil choice, but one that is a "lesser evil." Here lies Palpatine's braininess, which is present all the way from Episode I to Episode VI. Luke has to choose the Dark Side if he wants his closest friends to survive. It seems reasonable when Vader finds out about Leia's identity and provokes Luke by talking about recruiting her. It ends with the final death blow of Palpatine knowing everything about the supposedly great Luke's plan about deflector shields. The ultimate trolling done by Palpatine shows the tragic choice Luke faces: *Oh, I'm afraid you will be quite on the Dark Side when your friends arrive.* This ultimate confrontation is almost like that in a typical Greek tragedy. Whatever you choose, you will eventually lose (of course, the movie surprises us with a happy ending, but we'll discuss that later).

Containing the threats to his rule becomes an essential part of Palpatine's quest for ultimate dictatorial power. Fortunately for the living beings in the Empire, not everything transpires according to the Emperor's plan. Even the strongest, most wretched scum and villainy can fail when the right circumstances arrive.

Part Three: Fall of the Empire

IT STARTS WITH CHOICE

AFTER devoting a lot of space to explaining how totalitarian power arises, here we can elucidate its impressive downfall. How do such awful giants fall? How is unlimited power ultimately revealed to be not so unlimited? Naturally the meltdown has to start with a form of resistance—a conscious choice to secede from the oppressive regime. The imminent fall has to start with creating an opposing force. In *Star Wars*, this is a rebellion, whose seeds are presented in the deleted scenes of *Revenge of the Sith* (when Amidala promises to not tell her crazy lover about a political conspiracy between a couple of senators).

With the extreme confrontations between the dictatorial regime and the resistance, the two sides of the political spectrum refer to different notions of human existence (that does not need to always be the case, of course). As we have seen, in the example of the rising destructive Sithian power the narrative is that some form of *Geist* is directing everything. Historical forces have decided you have to lose. It is your destiny. The power of such deterministic statements comes also from a simple empirical fact: just look at who is winning the game. How can you even question the conqueror who managed to destroy all of the enemies? Just face the Goliath and bend your knee to admit his superiority. The Big Sithian Brother just has to be correct, right?

But it does not have to be this way, as none of human history is determined from the outset. Nothing inherent in human history guarantees the success or failure of peoples. Lots of revolutions and rebellions assume a certain something has to happen. The reality, especially in the case of opposition to totalitarianism, is that changes are happening because people are ready to make them happen. They have enough of the existing rulers and decide to fire them. What is the beginning of resistance? Hope, of course—a new hope. That title nailed it. As Andy Dufresne from *The Shawshank Redemption* inspiringly laments when thrown into the cellar: "There are places in this world that aren't made out of stone. That there's something inside ... that they can't get to, that they can't touch. That's yours. Hope."

People decide not to sit comfortably and instead decide to take a stand. Everyone makes a decision on his or her own. It's the same with our *Star Wars* heroes. Remember when Luke was called to action? We see this in one of the deleted scenes, when his friend decided to join the rebels and tried to convince him to do the same thing (he later met this friend in one of the original scenes very late in the movie). Obi-Wan issued another call to action by openly asking for help, which Luke ignored by noting that he hates the Empire but has other work to do. Obi-Wan did not push him, but mildly tried to persuade him, ending with the conclusion that he would do what he feels is right. *No pressure, kid. You have your free will. I fully respect that.*

Then the change happened. Luke became ready to join the opponents of the current order. A similar change happened to Han Solo, who at first had every reason to stay away from fighting the Empire—even more than Luke, as his life would be directly threatened. Luke is very much frustrated by Han's decision to not help him (eventually the story is turned around as we learn). When faced with Han's no, Leia reacts similarly to Obi-Wan and tells Luke that everyone has to find his own path. *Hey, kid, Han also has free will. Just respect that.*

Such small details perfectly demonstrate a massive philosophical clash between how the Empire recruits people and how the rebellion does. The former relies on political and historical necessity. The latter emphasizes sovereign individual choice. The Empire says it writes your history. The rebellion says you, and no one else, write your own history. Ultimately, that is the best way to win over people and truly convince them a cause is proper. Dedication to the truth and to moral obligations is strongest among free people. And the imminent collapse of the Empire has to start from a recognition of the necessity of choice.

Even though political revolutions are actively directed and executed by particular people, the public's support either for the regime or the revolution is a major factor here. We are used to thinking public opinion is important only in democratic systems, but it is not true at all. Public support always plays a role in legitimizing government, any government—be it democracy, monarchy, or oligarchy. People always have to passively support the regime in some way (sometimes they must give their passive support only because of the regime's horrifying means, of course).

A great French thinker, Étienne de La Boétie, was one of the first to demonstrate—very eloquently—that rulers' powers always come from public opinion. In his *Discourse on Voluntary Servitude*, he made strong statements that would later on be quoted by various thinkers:

> Poor, wretched, and stupid peoples, nations determined on your own misfortune and blind to your own good! You let yourselves be deprived before your own eyes of the best part of your revenues; your fields are plundered, your homes robbed, your family heirlooms taken away. You live in such a way that you cannot claim a single thing as your own; and it would seem that you consider yourselves lucky to be loaned your property, your families, and your very lives. All this havoc, this misfortune, this ruin, descends upon you not from alien foes, but from the one enemy whom you yourselves render as powerful as he is, for whom you go bravely to war, for whose greatness you do not refuse to offer your own bodies unto death.... Where has he acquired enough eyes to spy upon you, if you do not provide them yourselves? How can he have so many arms to beat you with, if he does not borrow them from you? The feet that trample down your cities, where does he get them if they are not your own? How does he have any power over you except through you? How would he dare assail you if he had no cooperation from you? What could he do to you if you yourselves did not connive with the thief who plunders you, if you were not accomplices of the murderer who kills you, if you were not traitors to yourselves?

By the way, this is a sixteenth-century piece. Very early on in the development of political thought, we have something basic about how power functions: power has to be accepted by the people. Naturally, Étienne is overstating the case to some extent. If someone puts a gun to your head, then it seems like a stretch to suggest you voluntarily accept that. Despite the stretch, Étienne does have a very relevant point: public support is a pillar for rulers. Often the support is not really voluntary. It can be elicited with aggressive means, but indeed it has to be there at some level.

The more people are harassed by the government, and the more they are treated like small parts of a machine to be started and stopped at the caprice of a ruler, the easier it is to undermine the government's support. The change has to come from within: insisting on the freedom of an individual becomes a major part of the *Star Wars* story's rebellion. Ultimately, freedom to choose becomes a higher virtue than making a particular choice. It is simply a value in itself.

While discussing political systems and legal architecture, it seems obvious we should focus on rules and institutions themselves. Despite the rightness of such an approach, ultimately it is the individuals that make choices and affect future events. The fundamental social tool embodying the approach is called methodological individualism: it means that only individuals make choices and act. Even when constrained by existing customs and legal instructions, the ultimate force behind the social order is human decisions to choose A or B.

Something that should not leave the picture is the fact that while making choices, people are not individuals completely isolated from the social rules. People are precisely the opposite. The environment in which they live bounds their actions and aims them in a particular direction. A great expert on and defender of methodological individualism, Ludwig von Mises, observed properly about humans:

> When he is born, he does not enter the world in general as such, but a definite environment. The innate and inherited biological qualities and all that life has worked upon him make a man what he is at any

instant of his pilgrimage. They are his fate and destiny. His will is not "free" in the metaphysical sense of this term. It is determined by his background and all the influences to which he himself and his ancestors were exposed.

Inheritance and environment direct a man's actions. They suggest to him both the ends and the means. He lives not simply as man in abstracto; he lives as a son of his family, his race, his people, and his age; as a citizen of his country; as a member of a definite social group; as a practitioner of a certain vocation; as a follower of definite religious, metaphysical, philosophical, and political ideas; as a partisan in many feuds and controversies. He does not himself create his ideas and standards of value; he borrows them from other people. His ideology is what his environment enjoins upon him. Only very few men have the gift of thinking new and original ideas and of changing the traditional body of creeds and doctrines.

The struggles of Luke, Han, and Lando are great demonstrations of the above social constraints. Luke, Han, and Lando generally hate the Empire. Yet that is not enough to get them to act. They are not isolated individuals. The decision is not so easy, as people are not abstract entities without any relation to what is happening around them. Luke has some work to do—take care of the farm—and it seems at first too costly for him to engage in a fight. Han would gladly help his new friends, but he has to survive Jabba's quest for his head. Lando truly hates the dark-helmeted man, but an offer he can't refuse is just too strong to refuse. Those attitudes soon reverse themselves. Luke does decide it is worth his while to fight the Empire. Han does decide his new friends really need his help. Lando does decide to stop being opportunistic and join the rebel movement.

If human beings were abstract entities, empires would fall very quickly. But they are not. They are involved in a myriad of dependencies and a net of social reliance such that it is very difficult to join the resistance. Individuals are not separated from the rest of society, but are very much tied to it and grounded in its customs. If the checks on resistance are so efficient, and the resistance needs Boétiean enlightenment to feed on, how does it even become possible to change the courses of events?

It happens through an tool that we all learned to love on the internet: memes.

IDEAS ARE LIKE MEMES

LET'S build upon something we know from the previous section: people's actions are grounded in their social surroundings. They believe in particular ideas partly because of the existing customs accepted by others. You can see this in the cases of political, religious, and cultural believers. In some places, it is usual for women to wear bikinis. In others, it is an outrage for them to show even their faces. In some places, offspring choose their own future mates. In other places, a daughter may be killed by a parent for doing so. These are simple examples, but the same goes for more sophisticated examples of thinking and philosophy. We are individuals, and we make decisions, but at the same time we have a natural tendency to simply copy other people. We choose whether to copy, and we choose whom we copy, but we still copy.

Nevertheless, there are "very few men having the gift of thinking new and original ideas and of changing the traditional body of creeds and doctrines." They are opinion leaders: people whom others follow because of their inspirational opinions and courageous actions. They are also meme creators.

How do memes work? Memes, a concept promoted by the biologist Richard Dawkins, are something different than genes. Genes are the programming building blocks of our bodies and contain information inherited from our ancestors. They determine many of our abilities and skills. They determine how we look. Despite their tremendous influence on our lives and their impressive informational content, however, they fall short of determining our lives. If a woman has identical twins, one placed in a middle-class family in New Zealand and another one in a middle-class family in Kiribati, after twenty years the two will be quite different. Why? Because other things in human beings' lives contribute to their outcomes besides biology. People as a species have developed the best possible tool to express additional information not contained in the genes: acquired language (the capacity for language itself is probably imprinted in our genes). Language is based on symbols that transmit an astonishing range of information: emotions, alliances, and eventually, knowledge (unfortunately, the first two may inhibit honest discussion, because people get emotional and tend to argue using ad hominems).

Memes are just means to transmit additional and important information. As Dawkins stated:

> Examples of memes are tunes, ideas, catch-phrases, clothes fashions, ways of making pots or of building arches. Just as genes propagate themselves in the gene pool by leaping from body to body via sperms or eggs, so memes propagate themselves in the meme pool by leaping from brain to brain via a process which, in the broad sense, can be called imitation....

> When you plant a fertile meme in my mind you literally parasitize my brain, turning it into a vehicle for the meme's propagation in just the way that a virus may parasitize the genetic mechanism of a host cell.

The second statement may be too strong, but it expresses the importance of copying and spreading information. For the Empire to collapse, a sufficient set of memes was necessary. There had to be an intellectual virus infecting people's thinking, one that constantly signaled to them there was something wrong with the current political system. Memes may take various forms. Since people do not really have a lot of imagination (contrary to many claims), one of the factors influencing them is stories about another, better world—either geographically distant or perhaps from a completely different time.

Once an oppressive regime is established and brought to life by aggressive means, people may start to ask themselves: Does it have to be this way? Is there no alternative? In the Soviet order, people knew of an alternative world: the so-called West. The contrast between worlds in the case of West and East Germany was especially strong. Despite having the same people and a similar culture, their social and economic results were completely different. One can of course imagine alternate worlds, but such a meme is not as powerful as imagining real-world alternatives. That is why other, empirically confirmed solutions work so well to capture people's minds and eventually become memes. People have to see something real to believe it. Han Solo's skepticism is the best example of this.

In some cases, geographical alternatives may not be available, as was apparently the case in *Star Wars*. There was just the lousy empire, which everyone had to live with. The people had historical points of reference, however. They got to share in the experiences of those who lived under the Old Republic and were still alive. And those who lived under the old regime quite well remembered that before Palpatinedom, things were not so bad. Their stories served as perfect material for generating memes and creating a call to action.

When Luke, Han, and Lando made their individual decisions to oppose the Empire, they did so because they were convinced by a combination of others' behaviors and some sequences of events. The rebellion was contagious. It had to be. People were attracted to it. It got into their brains and started to dominate their thinking. Luke heard stories about the old days of the Republic from Obi-Wan—stories about the Clone Wars and the Jedi serving in the Old Republic as peacekeepers (even though we learn from the prequel trilogy that a lot of Obi-Wan's stories were myths). Leia was brought up in a politically involved family, closely entangled in the rebellion and sharing her mother's ideological views. Her decision to fight an evil empire was catalyzed surely by her upbringing in an atmosphere of praise for the glory days of the Republic. People needed inspiration to take a stand against the Empire so they could fully realize the Boétiean message about passive support. Memes served precisely that purpose.

In his enjoyable book *The World According to Star Wars*, Cass Sunstein discusses the concept of information cascading, a part of decision-making theory. The idea of cascading comes from a spontaneous and organic process of people observing each other and changing their behavior based on their experiences. The most obvious form stems from the adoption of new technologies and inventions. Some people are the early testers, while most people couldn't care less. Some people started to use computer tablets, and they were a minority. But we observed them. We engaged in the process of understanding (*Verstehen*) what those individuals were doing: their motivations, exact goals, and the data guiding their actions. Through such observation and through interaction with them, other people are affected and adjust their decisions. When those other people try it, we have cascading. We should remember that cascading itself may be very fragile, and based on very little conscious thought. It can simply come from people's need to experiment (even irrationally) and swim against the tide. Many such experiments fade away. But some of them stay with us and change our social life fundamentally and forever. For beliefs and ideological views to cascade in this way, there need to be strong memes.

The spreading of the idea of a rebellion in the original trilogy is a wonderful example of solid cascading. Luke listened to his friends and received the advice of a great mentor, Obi-Wan. Luke was raised by a family offering him support and remembering about the possibility of a social order without Vader. Such surroundings created a fertile ground for the strong conviction to act against the Empire. He copied the behavior of Obi-Wan and Leia. His attitude to the Force and the revolutionary approach similarly inspired Han, who otherwise could not have cared less. Yet Han saw that other people he got to know and care for, Luke and Leia, were choosing to act in a specific way. Faced with a similar choice, he decided to give it a try and go along with the rebels. In this way, the idea memes created cascades, which became solid and stayed to create a strong, unified social movement.

Memes of course have to be transmitted. Personal contact and relations are often strong ways to influence other people. Nevertheless, the most efficient way to spread idea memes is through fast and large-scale channels of communication: books, papers, articles, speeches, radio, television, and the internet. Now you see the necessity for dictators to censor speech. It is not really that they dislike something—such as being made fun of (although that may well be the case too, given the sometimes psychotic nature of dictators). More importantly, channels of communication can efficiently build resilient idea memes. Empires and rulers are more prone to collapse when people fully realize their weaknesses: "The emperor has no clothes" are not just words in the wind. When the weakness becomes apparent, people may start laughing (overcoming their fear) and making fun of their rulers. Such signs mark the beginning of the end.

Let me be clear about the shortcoming of the meme metaphor. Metaphorically speaking, idea memes, which are firmly rooted in people's minds, may be seen as Dawkins's viruses repeated over and over again. Nevertheless, the spreading itself does not occur because a meme is some deterministic mechanism spreading across people's minds. What matters more is the ultimate power of the mind itself to spread content through communication. With people acting to communicate, it may look like cascading. And so a rebellion movement may very quickly spread through people's actions, thoughts, and symbols. That is why oppressive governments do everything to control messages and images, and the channels through which they are transmitted: to make themselves secure from potential uprisings.

THE INEFFICIENCY OF CENTRAL PLANNING

THE economy of the Empire is rarely, if ever, discussed in the original trilogy. Of course, "expanded universe" books provide details, but they are not always consistent with the movies. I prefer to stay with the films because the story of a fully nationalized economy subjected to military rule makes a lot of sense given the circumstances of Palpatinedom. Even the aesthetics fit the story. Every ship, building, and location is rough, cold, lacking creative artistic vision, and brutalist (in contrast to the colorful pictures from Episodes I–III). Economically, things appear to be the same way.

Zachary Feinstein wrote a brilliant article called "It's a Trap: Emperor Palpatine's Poison Pill," which describes the financial consequences of the Death Star's destruction. The compelling argument (one that can really teach you something about economics) is that the Death Star required sufficient funding through lending. Banks financed the Empire's investment. Once the Death Star was destroyed, we were left with a poison pill: the banking sector completely collapsed because of the necessary write-offs due to the lack of secure assets. It's somewhat like the case of the financial crisis of 2008 and thereafter, only on a much, much bigger scale. Feinstein did a great job of estimating how much the write-offs would have been. Because of a terrorist attack on the Death Star, many of these assets received a strong blow.

Nevertheless, there are major problems with such an argument. Firstly, an attack may actually boost assets. The 9/11 attacks were totally different from the attack on the Death Star. The former was a blow right into the heart of a market economy. The latter was a massive strike at the heart of a ruthless and oppressive leader's regime, where the leader was threatening basically everyone (a similar weapon in Episode IV destroyed an entire planet of productive people and other resources). Think about it: If some leader is expropriating investors, stealing from the public, and constructing ridiculously costly weapons that have absolutely no use for ordinary people, would getting rid of him enhance economic conditions or worsen them? How would business expectations be formed if people much more respectful of individual rights came into power?

Secondly, I take issue not just with the core argument, but with its presentation. Feinstein's article is based on the *Star Wars* universe and its portrayal of the banking and economic system. But this description stands in sharp contrast to the portrayal of the Galactic Empire in the prequel trilogy. Feinstein assumes the banking sector has some sovereignty, as is typical for a mixed economy, whereas under a real-world totalitarian regime the banks are like government bureaus. In the movies, the relationship between the Sith and the rest of the galaxy is a relationship based on commands, so it fits the second idea more. The Sith speak; the rest listen. If you do not listen, you will get choked. Such a military relationship is typical of centrally planned economies, not mixed economies. The above description of the Death Star is based on the idea of the Empire being a mixed economy with some amount of property rights and an independent financial sector. Clearly this is not what we learn from the movies. Palpatine does not care about having an independent financial sector. Do you really believe he bargained with the bankers? Do you really believe he applied to get the necessary credit score to receive funding? That sounds almost satirical. He gets what he wants, and if you are not ready to give to him, then he shall take it himself, or with a little help from the guy in the helmet.

So the Empire is probably a militarized, centrally planned economy, where property rights play a very limited role (even though the movies do not dwell on this much). At least, it should be so, as otherwise the resistance would have been much stronger. This is how the logic of advanced authoritarianism works: You can have your speeder, but the whole industry is being nationalized to serve the goals of the Emperor.

That is how you construct a Death Star: by going full Stalin, with top-to-bottom industrialization to create a war machine to terrorize people. Once the ownership of most resources is forcefully transferred to the monopolized power, the need for the financial sector simply disappears. If one entity controls all of the resources, who is there left to trade with? Itself? That would be absurd.

How was the imperial economy run, then? Unfortunately for the Sith, the Empire is very inefficient in its central planning. We learn this not all at once, but on three occasions: the building of a second Death Star, the smuggling by Han Solo, and the hiring of Boba Fett.

Vader was inspecting the building of the second Death Star when he threatened Jerjerrod, one of the chiefs responsible for the project. Notice Jerjerrod was a military man, which also confirms what we discussed above: the Empire has a military-planned centralized economy. Construction projects in a market economy (even in ones with a huge governmental role) are undertaken by civilians, not by the military, as the latter really does not have the proper background to manage such projects. But in an economy run fully by the state, the military becomes directly responsible. And yet despite its tremendous power, it still faces delays and cannot get its projects done on time—as is typically the case with real-world centrally planned economies, be they Soviet or some other type.

What does the profession of Han Solo tells us? He is a smuggler. With the help of a kind of mafia, he transports goods that are needed in various places in the galaxy. Apparently, shortages have arisen for important commodities. (It is not explicit what exactly is being smuggled, though the upcoming Han Solo movie will tell us.) As a result, gray and black markets have developed. This is also a typical weakness of centrally planned economies. Firstly, people lack products they need. The famous Hungarian economist János Kornai referred to socialist systems as based on the "economics of shortages." Secondly, entrepreneurs are not allowed to solve those shortage problems, as the only economic decision-making power lies in the hands of the ruler or his bureau. Typically, then, under central planning there is universal scarcity and the government outlaws the work of innovators who would eliminate it. Spot on, *Star Wars!* As Kornai states:

> I shall focus my attention on the problem of shortage. This is one of the central subjects in the economics of socialism [central planning]. The consumer constantly encounters shortage phenomena.... Tens of thousands are waiting to get a telephone station, or to buy a car. The gravest shortage phenomenon in consumption is a housing shortage which has grown into a pressing social problem. We keep encountering shortage phenomena not only as consumers but also as producers. Hindrances are not rare in the supply of materials, semi-finished products, and parts. Shortage of construction and installation capacity is conspicuous in investment processes. In addition to all this, labor shortage increasingly retards the expansion of production.... In my opinion all the above mentioned symptoms spring from the same root; in the final analysis they can be traced back to common main causes. We are faced with various concrete manifestations of the same general phenomenon. It is not a temporary, or occasional problem, but a chronic one with which we are faced. Certain social conditions, and certain properties of the economic mechanism discussed herein constantly reproduce shortage.

And those causal conditions, believe me, do not follow just from the bad intentions of the evil guy, the Emperor, and his right-hand man, whose vision is limited by his helmet. Ultimately, the flawed system rests on aggressive force, but the causes lie precisely in the nature of the oppressive system itself.

There is also the story of Boba Fett: a bounty hunter hired by the Empire to haunt down Han Solo. Seriously? An almighty empire with Darth Vader on the payroll is hiring a guy from the private sector to do military work? This is a clear red flag: *We can't handle the case. Help needed!* Yes, real-world despots cooperate with mafias and the underworld, but that just means their power is not as great and far-reaching as you may initially think.

When you are familiar both with the history of centrally planned economies and with sound economic theory, you can hardly be surprised by these three instances of the Empire's failure. Centrally planned economies are not efficient enough to catch smugglers, much as they are not efficient enough to finish construction projects on time—even when they threaten people. Most importantly, however, they fail in providing people with necessary goods and services. That is why the public has to rely on smugglers.

The main reason why an economy based on dictatorship cannot function well is that it abolishes the entrepreneurial class: a class of gifted people risking their own property to start and finish various promising (and risky) projects that may end up creating value for the population. Historian and economist Deirdre McCloskey, in her book *Bourgeois Dignity: Why Economics Can't Explain the Modern World*, eloquently describes the importance of a middle class for the economic development of any nation or country. As she noticed about the history of humankind:

> All ... changed on a large scale, first in Holland, in the Bourgeois Revaluation from the seventeenth through the nineteenth century. People needed to be persuaded to accept the outcome of innovation. It was a complicated cultural task, the creation of what the great economist Joseph Schumpeter, looking back with nostalgia from 1942 on Europe just before the First World War, called a "business respecting civilization." ... It became honorable—"Honorable!" the aristocrat snorts—to invent a machine for making screws or to venture in trade to Cathay.

In other words, if it is to flourish, society needs a respectable middle class composed of entrepreneurs and investors who are allowed to implement various technological and economic ideas. That at least has been true throughout the history of human civilization. Could there have been such a class under the Empire's rule? Hardly.

As you remember, in the Empire there could only be one power, an unlimited one, controlling all its territory. That explains its modus operandi very well. People's property was taken away, they were drafted into the army, and they were compelled to labor. This means there was no spontaneous labor market in which entrepreneurs were competing for workers, nor markets where other factors of production were being purchased. Everything was forced to comply with the big Sithian project. By destroying the entrepreneurial class, the Empire also destroyed all the possible innovative and sound economic ideas that could have led to efficient production. That is why the Empire was not capable of solving the problem of shortages. That is why a burdened, imperfect market developed and was run by smugglers.

When you analyze the history of the Soviet system, it really is all in there. Shortages were omnipresent, and smugglers developed ideas about how to hide their contraband packages so that officials wouldn't find them. Some of the Soviet governments were more brutal and determined than others to fight smugglers. In those cases, the standard of living was even lower for the population (interestingly, the more efficient the fight against the smugglers, the poorer the society). But it did not really matter. The point was to never allow anyone to question the efficiency of the Soviet system, and it was likewise with the Empire. Everyone had to repeat the lie. Otherwise, if people started to realize the Empire was wasteful, then anti-Empire memes would develop and spread across the population.

The same story applies not only to shortages, but big, impressive public projects. In theory, central plans were always prearranged to be hyperefficient and to reach 100 percent of their goals. In reality of course, plans were rescheduled, not completed on time, and were often worthless even when they were completed. But the ministry of propaganda had to tell the public: *Everything is under control. Situation normal. Maybe a slight construction malfunction, but, uh, everything's perfectly all right.* Denial was the foundation of the economically failing giant.

From an economic standpoint, in other words, the collapse of the Empire was inevitable. Its inefficiencies were bound to pile up. By wiping out the competitive aspects of a market economy, and by introducing political rule over the whole of galactic society, the consequences were simple and predictable: the military with all its powerful and technologically impressive weaponry could not be a substitute for creative entrepreneurs. The Sith thought like many real-world socialist rulers did: *If a problem appears, I will just decree that the problem has to disappear. Just in case, I've got guns, I've got people, I've got everything.* Does it work? No. What you don't have, what you need for the economy to be innovative and efficient, are Bezoses, Jobses, Zuckerbergs, Pages. You just killed them or expropriated them, Ani. In your foolishness, you failed to foresee the destructive effect on value creation.

Now, even though the Empire had a built-in tendency to fail (ironically, similar to the first Death Star), it does not follow it actually had to fail. Ideological factors were necessary. Despite its catastrophic harvests, the Soviet system managed to function through almost the entire twentieth century. Constant failure, however big, does not guarantee that a regime will be stopped. People can be trapped into making a similar mistake over and over again. Nevertheless, the economic tendencies were undeniable and explain why economic problems developed despite the Sith's powers.

Passive Opposition Must Penetrate the Empire

Economic conditions generated suitable conditions for the Sithian economy to collapse, but as we've discussed, ideological changes needed to alter the actions of real people. We need and get heroes, whom we root for with passion. But following the thoughts of de La Boétie, we can question how the masses react to the political reshuffling. Do they stand behind the Empire, or the rebels who are ready to fight it? The last scene of *Return of the Jedi* shows that people are quite happy with the fall of the Empire. Somewhat secretly, everyone wants the Empire to collapse and is fed up with the dictatorial rule.

In collapses of political orders, three factors must coincide. Firstly, people need alternate leaders who pave the way for change. Secondly, people must at least passively and quietly support these alternate leaders. Thirdly, the opposition needs its supporters within the regime. It would be difficult to take over without such support.

The first and most obvious case of the opposition within is Darth Vader himself. Did you know he was Luke's father? When you think about it, that is one of the most brilliant lines in the whole series. There is much more to it than just a simple soap opera connection. It adds to the reasons why *The Empire Strikes Back* may be the best of all the *Star Wars* movies: the "bad" guys are regular human beings. Not only are they real people. They are our brothers, sisters, mothers, fathers. They are flesh, bones, emotions, family members. They are not soulless machines. Yes, they have minds and values that make them our enemies. Even so, they are still members of the same species. Believe it or not, every human monster we know from history was still a human.

A New Hope was shallow in its portrayal of the universe (but we cannot really blame it, as it merely introduced the *Star Wars* universe). The good guys were nice, fun, and compassionate. They had a sense of humor and were likable. The bad guys were hidden inside uniforms, so we did not get to see their individual features. They were merely following orders like programmed machines. The person giving orders was basically a machine, not man. And, of course, those soulless machines have to lose at the end when the good guys save the day. Hooray!

The Empire Strikes Back does away with all that. As sympathizers to the Force we get a major shock. First, the bad guys are winning. We learn that the world is a nasty place, and the good side is never guaranteed to win. Bad guys usually have more tools and do not play by the rules, so they get the advantage. But second, those bad guys are also human. That is why "I am your father" is such a devastating revelation. It goes against our primitive instincts to portray the people on the other side as inhuman. There is a wonderful YouTube video showing kids' reactions to the final scene in *The Empire Strikes Back*. Go and watch it, it's captivating. Their responses will tell you everything about the importance of the scene. Virtually all of them take Luke's position: "That's not true. That's impossible!" Oh really? Did you forget which species was responsible for creating the regime?

It is the people who create oppressive governments. It is the people who commit genocide. It is the people who slaughter women and children. Bad guys are not sent from hell. They are members of the same species. The original sin lies deeply in us.

That is of course the dark side of the whole story. But hope is never lost. People on the other side of the fence can change. You can convince them to choose the alternate way—always. No human being, however bad, is ever too far gone. Admittedly, bringing them back may require taking a thorny and unacceptable path, but we may at least try. That is also a good lesson about the power of argumentation. People get emotional, and they use language most of the time not for reasoning, but for solving practical problems—and justifying support for their own tribe. But since the mind always has the ultimate say, there is always the possibility of opening a discussion. Opening a discussion may prove to be important for a behavioral shift. Vader's case represents one such instance.

Also, one should remember the chain of command in the military system. Someone must give orders to the military to go on fighting, to eliminate the enemy. Members of the military might have brothers and sisters who do not like the Empire. An army official might go home, see his rebel-sympathizing children, talk to his Empire-hating wife, and feel worse and worse about following orders. The only thing that keeps him going are strong and clear commands from the chief. But if the chief disappeared, then the official would happily abstain from putting an order into full force.

We could have gotten a glimpse of this in *Star Wars*, but unfortunately, the scenes depicting this kind of event were deleted. In an underrated story in *Return of the Jedi*, we hear more about Commander Jerjerrod, who was responsible for building the second Death Star. Later on, he also manages operations against the Rebellion. In the most important deleted scene, he receives an order from the Emperor: destroy Endor. He is hesitant to follow it though, as he knows of stationary imperial units there, in addition to the Rebel units (the Emperor doesn't care and is ready to sacrifice his soldiers). The actor who plays Jerjerrod portrays hesitance spectacularly, though that is not surprising since he was one Shakespearean actor among several in *Star Wars*. They are always the best. Why do you think people love Tarkin and Palpatine so much?

Back to the point: the Empire's army is not only being defeated, but is also falling apart from the inside. If (contrary to fact) Jerjerrod uses a comlink to confirm the order, he will hear only silence. *Emperor, are you there? Repeat, are you there? Should we commence fire? ... I'll contact Vader then. Darth Vader, are you there? I repeat, are you there? Should we start to fire?*

The collapse of the oppression from within is dazzlingly portrayed in the dystopian film *V for Vendetta*. During the climax, a bunch of unarmed people simply start to walk toward the parliament building, which is surrounded by an army of tanks, guns, and military officers that could easily wipe them out in a second. Yet no bullet is fired. Not a single person is killed. People walk by the army, and the soldiers just stand there. Why? Because the higher-ranked officer doesn't give an order. Why? Because he didn't get an order from higher officials, who in turn didn't receive one from the highest officials (as they were already taken down by the vigilante).

I must admit I absolutely love that scene even though it's unfaithful to the graphic novel (which is much smarter than the movie, by the way). One reason to like it though—besides being inspiring and charming—is that it isn't contrary to the real world. During the Communist era in Europe, there was that thing called *the wall*. No, I do not mean that excruciating Pink Floyd album about its leading man's internal pain. I mean the Berlin Wall, which symbolized the division of Germany between East Germany (Communist) and West Germany (not Communist). After the Second World War, millions of people ran away from the Eastern side to join the better world on the Western side. The Eastern government did everything it could to stop them. Building the wall was one such means. The story of that edifice includes many tragic moments, with people being killed by the military while trying to get to the other side.

In any case, back in November 1989 the wall was finally destroyed. Before that, a series of events led to the slow meltdown of the Soviet Empire, and some loosening in the migration policy of East Germany. So change was in the air, but it came faster than expected. Someone inside the regime proposed a new, softer law to allow the people to travel with faster-issued permits, and a member of an East German political bureau mistakenly (intentionally?) said at the associated press conference that the law would be put in place without a delay and the people could simply go to the other side of the wall. You can guess where it went from there. After hearing this everywhere on the news, thousands of people immediately went to the wall to travel—even though the law was not in place and it wasn't even very liberal. The guards were not instructed to let the people through. But faced with the crowd pushing them, they had two choices: capitulate or slaughter thousands of civilians. And so the very same army that just months earlier shot civilians trying to escape decided not to pull the trigger. Since no one gave orders to shoot, no one fired, and the rest was history: people tore down the wall and David Hasselhoff stood on it to sing his song "Looking for Freedom." No, that's no joke, he almost got hit by a firework while doing that. Twice! (Meanwhile, BBC reporters had a Monty Python–like discussion).

The moral of the story is that passive opposition catalyzed the fall of the unwanted regime. Back in the 1980s, some of the Communist Party leaders in Poland were fed up with central planning as they themselves were experiencing economic problems. They could not immediately buy a washing machine or a bathtub. Even though they were in a much better position than most of Polish society, they easily saw that despite being members of the elite, their living standards were comparable to the lowest of the middle class in the West. Such observations boosted anti-regime sentiments within the regime itself.

Rogue One makes the general point even clearer. Galen Erso comes to be dissatisfied with the Empire and actively works inside it to stop the monstrous power of the Death Star. So does his pilot. The whole structure of all four movies about the Empire's collapse shows how passive opposition is necessary to speed change in the government. *Call out the instigators, because there's something in the air. The Empire shall fall sooner or later, because the revolution's here, and everyone knows it's right.*

THE EMPIRE CANNOT BE DEFEATED BY THE DARK SIDE

FACE it: Luke is an honest but naïve kid. As often happens, those two qualities go together. His naivety pushes him to confront his dark father and the Emperor. Both Obi-Wan and Yoda are well aware of his weakness and at one point want to stop him from confronting Vader. At the same time, Luke's honesty allows him to make the most courageous choice of all: to die honestly rather than live immorally. It's a daring choice that in the real world very few people follow.

A sad aspect of *Return of the Jedi* is that hardly anyone pays much attention to the dilemma Luke faces and the tragedy of his decision. The simple explanation is that by making a moral and audacious judgment, Luke becomes a winner. He is an underdog, and to our complete surprise he prevails. Unfortunately, we just take it for granted, but that makes the whole story seem trivial and his sacrifice almost unimportant. Who would ever face genuine ethical dilemmas if going with the proper choice yielded the best possible results most of the time? If good always meant winning, what would the challenge be? Only a completely irrational person would be willing to become a bad person. In real life, the problem in sinning that often leads to winning.

Luke's story confirms this truth. Let us recall the circumstances. He appears to have become a truly powerful master of the Force, yet we are taught that his powers stem from anger and hate, the engines of the Dark Side. At the moment when Vader lies on the ground defeated, Palpatine instructs Luke: "Fulfill your destiny and take your father's place at my side." Luke then realizes that the powers he gained were of evil origins. Perhaps he can defeat the Emperor in a fight, but only by using the Dark Side of the Force. Instead, he passes, while sending a clear signal: "I'd

95

rather die than join you." Oh, that is quite powerful. We all have it in our heads years after seeing the movie.

Luke's stand would seem to inevitably produce three unfortunate consequences: the near annihilation of the Rebellion, the death of Luke's friends, and his own death. He was going to pay the price for his lack of vision. Despite Luke being in a seemingly losing position, suddenly the tide changes, and Anakin—obviously touched by Luke's words "like my father before me"—decides to go back. His choice overshadows everything else in the scene, so it becomes canonical—which is kind of upsetting when you think about it, since the main protagonist of the first-released trilogy is thus downplayed. Luke has just decided to be the bravest person in the galaxy: he refused to join Mr. Evil, or perhaps even take his place, because he didn't believe in using evil means to achieve his goal, despite knowing fully about the consequences. That is what we call moral courage—its pure essence.

Palpatine is shocked and even insulted. The ultimate puppet master, the trickiest rat in the galaxy, the most prescient politician around has been proven absolutely wrong, and the universe has failed to follow his Hegelian story. Not everything can go as planned. Not every single aspect of human choice can be controlled. Palpatine becomes so angry about Luke's choice that he even gets carried away in the pleasure of torturing him and forgets the possibility Anakin will shift back to the other side of the Force. Vader is even more astounded. He had chosen the Dark Side for personal reasons influenced by images seen in his dreams. Luke was in a similar position, but in a more tragic way, as he would not only lose all his family and friends, but witness the deaths of millions of others. Let's be honest: Luke was facing something much worse than Anakin. Despite being pushed further though, he resisted more than his father did. What father would not have been impressed with a son like that?

Again, it's a magnificent and significant choice, but we fail to see it as such because Vader's conversion stands out more and is an essential part of the ending of the film. It is sort of like the parable of the prodigal son.

Why care about the one who was always there, whom we can always trust, and of whom we know what to expect, when the other son—who always disappointed us—gives us a positive surprise? Now, we may be being a bit unfair. In the end, the always good son rises above his ego, and so it is the case with Luke; but the father is no longer Darth, and that seems most important. But should we really see the characters' choices this way?

Setting aside the overwhelming importance of the conversion, however, what remains to be emphasized is a truly Tolkienian move on Luke's part. In *The Lord of the Rings*, the wisest of the wise, and the strongest of the strong, who are well aware of the dangers, decide not to use the ring of power. They know perfectly well how corruptive it is, how addictive it is. They realize that good intentions and moral goals would not make the ring moral, and would only cloud their own rational assessments. Luke is in exactly the same position, and in his own way rises to the level of Gandalf: *Power? No, thank you. I know how poisonous it is. It intoxicates your thinking, then your actions, and ultimately it is lethal to the people you're trying to help.*

Luke throwing away his lightsaber in the final scene is like throwing away the ring of power. You do not defeat the devil by becoming one. What you must do is refuse, as in the underrated movie *The Devil's Advocate*. Free will is as delicate as butterfly wings. Cherish it properly or else you'll give in to something that makes you the slave of someone else.

Do you know the main problem with political revolutions against oppressive regimes? They often end up changing the staff in charge without the changing the substance of the government. Different people, different faces, but business as usual. People in post-Communist countries often joke about how much needs to be changed so that nothing really changes—especially when ruling becomes a regular job at which one can earn a good amount of money. Money and privilege are the best things for politicians, aren't they? New people coming into office will slightly alter some things, but the new people will still carry on with many of the disastrous policies of the older rulers. In *Star Wars*, the Sithian disease has disastrous consequences as it spreads to other organizations. The more corrupt the government becomes, the more corruption gets treated as a regular way of handling things. Why do you think changes in so many societies are so hard to realize? Because bad governments are like cancer. Their negative effects spread to everyday activities and become part of the socio-political culture. Merely changing the people in power cannot reverse that. Something much deeper is needed for a true shift in outcomes.

I must pause here and contemplate some of the alternate endings of *Return of the Jedi*. As we learn from interviews, some unhappy versions of the ending were considered in order to shock the viewers. No, I don't mean Han Solo's death on Endor (and who cares about Harrison Ford's obsession with killing the character he played?). I mean the option where Luke decides to turn to the Dark Side. Yes, apparently it was considered, although ultimately Lucas decided to go with the happy ending. How would Luke go about abandoning his beliefs? Either by killing his father and joining the Dark Side like Palpatine suggested; or by putting his father's helmet on after the clash between Vader and the Emperor, when his father dies in his arms. Just picture that for a moment: Vader thanks his son and exits, and then Luke starts to wear the helmet and decides to crush the Rebellion and introduce his own rule in the galaxy. That would finally bring peace and restore order, right?

Shocking? Possibly. But how realistic it would have been. Ruling becomes a tempting choice. For most rulers it becomes almost an obsession—exactly like the ring of power. During the final duel in Episode VI, Luke realizes that by using the Dark Side, he is not overthrowing the Empire, but actually sustaining it and supporting its methods. The only way to defeat the Empire is to let it wither away, or to get rid of it—not to reform it, not to change the staff, but simply to abolish it. Everyone leaves the building immediately, the last one out turns off the lights. Goodbye, Palpatine. Your ambitious project has just been defeated by the simple refusal of the most moral man in the universe.

PART FOUR: FURTHER REFLECTIONS ON POWER

Hazards of Power: Jedi Are Dangerous Too

NOW is the time to consider some remaining problems. In particular, it's time to consider the Jedi, or should I say, time to consider this pompous and blinded sect that participated so unwittingly in the destruction of the Old Republic. All right, I exaggerate to some extent.

In the original trilogy, we learned about the Jedi from Obi-Wan and Yoda. So we only get to hear from the main representatives of the organization, who, unsurprisingly, depict it almost as if it consisted entirely of angels. We have every reason to assume Obi-Wan and Yoda are romanticizing something to which they devoted their lives. Would you expect two founding fathers of any political party to fundamentally criticize it? Yoda and Obi-Wan, however nice, however smart, may be considered propagandists of the Jedi brand. They must promote good public relations to recruit new people—in our case, Luke.

Perhaps they are telling the truth, but we have every reason to be at least skeptical of how they judge their own organization. The prequel trilogy rightly proves we should always be cautious when evaluating people's accounts of their own history and flaws. Consider all the dubious choices we see the Jedi masters make. The first and most surprising one is made by Qui-Gon Jinn in Episode I, who actually makes a whole series of shocking decisions (in part because he has very bad intuition). For example, we see him use Jedi mind tricks to steal. Firstly, he steals a ship from the Gungans. He doesn't use physical force, but he uses a Jedi mind trick to fool someone into making poor use of their private property. That really is no different from simple theft. The mind trick was used originally in Episode IV by Obi-Wan to get away from oppressive soldiers who would have confiscated him droids and arrested him. It was certainly a noble goal to fight off the extensive Palpatinean Patriot Act. As Obi-Wan taught us: *You do not have the right to ask for identification: these droids aren't yours. People are free to go on with their business. Move along!*

Unfortunately, Qui-Gon does not use his powers to defend himself from oppression, but to take advantage of other people. He becomes a thief undisciplined by the Jedi council. At another point in Episode I, he tries to steal a hyperdrive generator by offering its owner some useless currency of the Republic (possibly inflationary, as it is far from "something more real"). Fortunately, the salesperson is smart enough to realize his intention. In the end, why does Qui-Gon bother at all with trying to cheat like this? How about just stealing the generator during the night? What difference would that make, morally? None.

The moral issues get even more troublesome, since the Jedi master decides to take a boy from his mother and leave her in the hands of the slave owner. This is absolutely unethical. Also, as we know from the dialogue between Amidala and Shmi Skywalker, even from a legal standpoint slavery is no longer acceptable in the galaxy. Qui-Gon then has every reason not to respect the slave owner's claim on any other living being. Despite such obvious moral facts, he decides not to do anything about the slavery. He is ready to steal a ship and a key component of it, and to cheat in a game of chance, but he does not fulfill his moral obligation to defend an enslaved woman. Nothing else about Qui-Gon is as shocking as this. He is ready to take away others' physical property, but not their immorally and illegally "owned" people.

Perhaps this was only a mistake by a single Jedi. After all, we know that Qui-Gon often defied the council and acted on his own judgment. He even believed in the pseudo-science of midi-chlorian counts, which clearly violated Yoda's teaching. (Yes, believe it or not, what Qui-Gon said about those midi-chlorians should not be accepted as the mainstream knowledge of the Jedi. It could well have been a minority view of some Jedi nut challenging everyone else. I bet Qui-Gon was also against vaccines.) Maybe he was merely a black sheep of the Jedi. If this was the case though, then we at least deserve some commentary in reaction, some discipline from his supervisors: *Why on earth did you not free his mother?* Instead, we hear silence, which looks like confirmation. It looks as if it's business as usual for the Jedi to take children away from their parents, while not caring at all about those parents.

The whole way of training and raising Jedi confirms this in a quite disturbing way. The council is obsessed with recruiting children under a certain age in order to fully direct their lives and raise them. (This is notably mentioned even in the original trilogy. Luke is far too old to be trained, remember? Too old for what? Brainwashing?) This is a signature of a very sectarian approach: Draft the youngest people possible before they develop their independent thinking and fear of death, before they fall in love, before they get a taste of regular life. Put messy and underdeveloped stoic stories into their heads so they can only think within such a framework, and they'll become ready to follow their leaders. Naturally, I am overstating the case a bit, since we see the council relies on discussion, not the cult of a leader. However, their approach to children is problematic and even mindboggling. It makes you think twice about what they do. Remember Anakin's discussion with Amidala about democracy? His views on the political process are so narrow that they indicate his complete lack of knowledge about the issues of power and governing. It's another confirmation of how backward the Jedi education system is. You would expect much more understanding by Padawans of what government is, what ruling means, and why governance is important. After all, the Jedi are part of that system of power and they are supposed to protect the galaxy from people who threaten it. They should know its nature well. What do all those younglings get taught in school? Did Anakin fall asleep during his philosophy and politics courses, or is the program mainly focused on having fun with lightsabers with Yoda clapping? They learn the biology of living beings, but do not care about the fundamentals of society? Do they receive public funding only for the natural sciences, or what?

Consider some equally important political questions about the Jedi's governmental powers. They officially are a special service serving the senate by "keeping the peace." We learn they cannot fight a war because that is not the Jedi way. Yet Episode II contradicts this supposed fact. The Jedi are engaged on a huge battlefield. They play a role in the formation of the clone army. Oh Yoda, what have you done? The Jedi have contributed to cloning of human beings, who are trained, raised, and brainwashed to become killing machines, blindly serving the state in the process. We cannot just forget this. This aggression will not stand, man.

On top of all this, they are incapable of handling the problem of how to limit power. Even though they are to fight for checks and balances, when faced with a crisis they break their own rules. Firstly, they abstain from reporting to the senate that their power is diminished. Secondly, instead of arresting Palpatine—as they should—Mace Windu decides to assassinate him. That is certainly not consistent with their code. The justification is also dubious: "Too dangerous to be kept alive"? Just imagine that Windu stayed faithful to the rules. Anakin wouldn't have killed him, and Palpatine would have been arrested. The whole dynamic would have changed, especially with Yoda back in the capital city. But no, the temptation of gaining more power proves to be too strong. Windu makes a tragic decision that contributes to the destruction of society. And don't even start with all that Anakin nonsense about the Jedi's power to act for "the common good." It only made Palpatine laugh. It did not work on Amidala. It will not work on me. If you want more on the failure of the label "good guys," see the next chapter.

In the end, the Jedi are an army of a growing superpower, a bureaucratic entity struggling for a position in the system—another thing Lucas got perfectly right about the way of the Jedi in the prequels. He presented some of those dubious choices to demonstrate the corrupt nature of power. No matter who has it, power is a dangerous tool. Angels are not among us. Anyone can be a threat when in power, even Gandalf. Some of course are bigger threats than others, but the threat is always there. Jedi are really not that different. When they take the power of the ring, it corrupts their thinking. Though of course not a Jedi, Amidala seems to be the only person who stays faithful to her principles (even though she clearly makes some political mistakes). The Jedi are also silent on the pressing issue of attacking the separatists. They are actually quietly supporting the increasingly powerful regime and a form of imperialism: forced obedience to the central body. Why do they not stand up and respect people's right to offer different views, like Amidala's, in the senate during the debate on the use of military force (this occurs in a deleted scene)? They should be loudly and proudly fighting for that goal, just as they also should be freeing the slaves around the galaxy. But apparently that is not for them. Therefore their value system may be challenged on many levels.

One last embarrassing fact about the Jedi: Luke wins in the end because he is not a Jedi. He decides not to listen to either Yoda or Obi-Wan. He relies on his positive emotions and empathy for others (something missing in the Jedi philosophy, apparently)—both when he decides to help Han and Leia (Yoda tells him he should stay), and when he decides not to kill his father (rejecting Obi-Wan's proposal). Remember Kenobi's reaction when Luke declares he will not kill Vader? If Luke fails to do so, "then the Emperor has already won." Not only is a Jedi knight committing a mistake, but a dead Jedi knight is committing a mistake. How can the ghost of a good guy be wrong (apparently living in some form of Jedi heaven)? Luke is a Jedi revolutionary. He questions the whole premise of Jedi philosophy, decides to go a different way than the Jedi suggest. He takes hope and a leap of faith in believing in the strength of catharsis.

In the end, the Jedi get on by spying, war mongering, confiscating property, accepting slavery, serving the imperial state, questioning the limits of their power and others' right to a fair trial, and kidnapping children. If these are the guardians of peace that Obi-Wan in talks about in Episode IV, then I guess I missed something. The reality is that George Lucas wins again with an accurate portrayal of the hazards of power, which corrupts everyone.

HAZARDS OF POWER: THE REBELS ARE DANGEROUS TOO

How do you know the rebels are the good guys? How do you make the right moral judgment about who should win the war? That seems very easy when you look at the original trilogy. The good guys are smiling, empathetic, likable, and handsome and have a sense of humor. The bad guys are virtually faceless machines following orders to destroy, destroy, destroy. And conquer. They even have names clearly indicating their badness: Darth Vader, the Dark Side, the Death Star. Yet is that really the reason the rebels are the team we should root for? Because someone is using a simple, straightforward trick? *Look here, dummy! These are the bad guys!*

One of the hitches is that in real-life ideological conflicts, one side often tries to portray the other as horrid, distasteful, inhuman, primitive, stupid, and ugly. One should not have any trouble in finding such cases. An active Republican will often find the most radical Democrat to demonstrate how awful Democrats are. An active Democrat will do the same thing with Republicans. Find the worst representative possible, find the weakest and the most repulsive member of the other herd, and you can start your propaganda to completely discredit the other herd. If Vader was vegan, then all vegans must be evil, right? Something is wrong with us human beings, because we just love to think in those categories, even if the groups we're part of are not biological. Focus on someone, put them in a drawer, label them, and then attack viciously the whole group. Look at sports. Listen to Real Madrid and FC Barcelona fans discussing how nasty the fans of the other side are. There is a crazy fan somewhere, so why would you ever want to like the same thing as that guy? How about in *Star Wars*? Do I need to go into specifics?

Check out the online arguments about the prequels.

Foolish as it may sound, the trick works on our limited minds, so it is actually effective. We must face the brutal fact of our own silliness in labeling people like this and acting in a tribal way when organizing society. Let us be honest with each other: we tend to immediately judge strangers when we find out who they voted for. It's even true of intelligent people, because intelligence does not guarantee being unbiased. Yes, intelligent people are also keen on not listening and on being fixated on their established views. They have more intellectual means to be open-minded, but having the means and using them are radically different things. Intelligence is also a matter of choice. Nobody is forced to use it. You can decide to abstain from using your brain, no matter how smart you are. This should not come as a surprise, since similar processes are happening in your brain when you are physically attacked or when someone merely questions your views. Instinctively, we treat both acts as violations, and our immediate response seems to be self-defense—even when we may be wrong. Only later on, after calm reflection, may we realize that perhaps some thinking could be useful to extending our knowledge. You can trust Yoda on this: "You will know ... when you are calm, at peace, passive."

As the great social psychologist Jonathan Haidt (you definitely should read his wonderful book on these topics entitled *Righteous Mind*) stated: "Social reality is so complicated that, once you join one team or the other, you become specialized in detecting certain patterns, but you become blind to other patterns.... Politics is really religion. Politics is about sacredness. Politics is about offering a vision that will bind the nation together to pursue greatness."

Well said. The *Star Wars* story goes along the same lines. We are supposed to root for the apparently better side, because simple forms of propaganda tell us to. We are here to reflect on whether we actually should. *Rogue One* opens a new chapter in understanding the whole religion side of the story. All rebel soldiers are expected to join the movement and blindly demonstrate almost a religious commitment—

because they are the good guys. Right.

Let me tell you something about the "good guys" label by mentioning again an innovative TV series: *Lost*. Consider an exchange between one of the characters—Michael—and Benjamin Linus, the leader of a strange group called the Others. After a series of morally questionable actions on the part of the Others, Michael asks Linus who they really are. Linus responds impeccably: "We are the good guys, Michael!" It is almost like something Walter White from *Breaking Bad* would say: *Do not worry. Everything is okay. We are doing a good thing.*

Another character in the series later on reacts with pure gold to the quote—not just because he is questioning the idea that the Others are "the good guys," but because he makes a great comment on using the label: "In my experience, the people who go out of their way to tell you they're the good guys are the bad guys." In other words, if someone takes the effort to tell you he is good—so good—then perhaps that is a red flag. It is not who you are underneath, nor what you say, but what you do that defines you, as Batman would say. You demonstrate your goodness by your actions, not by spouting hot air, not by labeling yourself "good." We should take the same approach to understanding the actions of our heroes. Overusing the labels "good" and "bad" is part of the reason why Nietzsche started to question the value of the distinction.

Rogue One presents us with a lot of dubious characters and strongly breaks away from a clear-cut moral distinction between the Empire and the rebels. Cassian Andor is on the side of rebels, but he is far from an angel (early on we see that he kills off his informant). He uses an extreme and weak way of justifying many of his morally dubious actions:

> Some of us—well, most of us—we've all done terrible things on behalf of the Rebellion. Spies, saboteurs, assassins. Everything I did, I did for the Rebellion. And every time I walked away from something I wanted to forget, I told myself it was for a cause that I believed in. A cause that was worth it. Without that, we're lost. Everything we've done would have been for nothing. I couldn't face myself if I gave up now. None of us could.

I already talked about the brilliant element in *The Empire Strikes Back* as compared to *A New Hope*. The latter was almost primitive in its depiction of good and evil. We can understand that. The point was to establish the basic laws of the universe. There was no time to go into more nuance in a two-hour movie. Then the next episode struck us with the magnificent revelation "I am your father," which reminded us that bad guys are still real living beings. They think, they react; they are not programmed machines, but flesh and bones with different moral views.

How do we know then which is the good side, or which side is not? Of course, by ignoring simple symbols we get more of the story. We can learn from sequences of choices who the good people are—surely not the ones who are destroying whole planets and killing innocent people. But beware, and do not be fooled. Lucas's simple story has some hidden warnings. Obviously, the prequel trilogy contains one such warning. The world of the Old Republic is not as simple as it is in the Palpatinedom story. We see things are far from perfect. More than that, we see that the good guys are making tremendous mistakes and dubious choices. The older trilogy does not dwell on that, because it is a story of vindicated heroism against the Darth Goliath. There is an excellent book called *The Hero with a Thousand Faces*, written by Joseph Campbell, that clearly influenced Lucas in writing the original trilogy. Campbell shows convincingly that many hero stories are built in a similar manner, and with similar elements, including a call to adventure, a series of trials, a change, and a return. We have all that in the original *Star Wars* trilogy, so unsurprisingly not much is devoted to exploring the nature of the conflict. Lucas made it shallow so we could focus on a more personal story.

Hence, the reason why *A New Hope* offers such underdeveloped views of the two sides in the conflict. It is more about personal development and maturing, not about general philosophy. But you can find some hidden brilliance in the over-the-top description of the easily recognizable good rebels versus the bad imperial state. I am talking about the pompous ending scene of Episode IV in the throne room—yes, the distasteful one in which Chewie does not receive a medal, the one in which there are lots of smiles, great music, and overall amusement of the rebels. Do you know what that scene is mimicking? A scene from one of Leni Riefenstahl's movies, *Triumph of the Will*.

Riefenstahl was a Nazi propaganda director. *Triumph* is her most famous work. You can go to YouTube and watch a magnificent interplay between the ending of Episode IV and her movie (search for "triumph of the new hope"). It will demonstrate to you that the film tools used in both scenes are quite similar: close-ups of the faces of the officers, looking proud; strong masculine symbols both in the architecture of the building and in the standing army; a perfectly organized military ready to immediately respond to military commands.

The scene reaches its cartoonish height so it can make fun of itself without many viewers noticing. After all, the creators' point was not to show that the rebels are fascists. The point was that any society may be threatened by dictatorial manipulation of the masses. It is very easy to influence people and lure them into liking the rulers without hesitation and reflection (again, in *Rogue One*, blind devotion is quite visible and may be disturbing to a more reflective audience). That is how propaganda works, and that is why it is always dangerous. It could happen in any society. We learn this in detail in the prequels, but we also have this message in code in the ending of Episode IV. The depiction of the political spectrum is so watered down that it finally becomes its own caricature and defeats itself.

In other words, the final scene of *A New Hope* sounds like what's called Wittgenstein's ladder. Ludwig Wittgenstein was one of the most important philosophers of the twentieth century. He wrote a short, ingenious book on philosophy using clearly defined concepts and perfectly logical structure, all in order to reject most of philosophy. He realized that by doing so, in the end he was undermining himself, which you can see in one of the last theses: "My propositions serve as elucidations in the following way: anyone who understands me eventually recognizes them as nonsensical, when he has used them—as steps—to climb beyond them. (He must, so to speak, throw away the ladder after he has climbed up it.) He must transcend these propositions, and then he will see the world aright."

The ending scene of *A New Hope* serves a similar purpose. It draws on a piece of Nazi propaganda to clandestinely show how people can be manipulated through good feelings and loyalty to a group. To summarize the lesson to be learned from the picture: do not rely on tribal emotions, do not fall for the smiles, do not fall for fictitious order, do not fall for labels. Reason is the only weapon to properly assess the appropriateness of actions. Without reason, the rebels ultimately become as dangerous as the Empire itself, no less treacherous than all those senators from the Old Republic that accepted the death of liberty with thunderous applause.

HUMAN FAULT OR INSTITUTIONAL ERROR?

WHO killed the Republic? Was it really all Palpatine's (or Darth Plagueis's) fault? Is it really true that the Empire conquered the Republic? Perhaps George Lucas is right, and the Empire *is* the Republic?

The question is not a trivial one about a movie plot, but a serious one for the political sciences. To what degree can we put the blame on a particular person? After the Second World War, the Nuremberg trials tried to identify each of the main Nazi officers' amount of guilt. I am sure a similar project would make perfect sense after the first six episodes of *Star Wars*—I guess we could call them the Alderaan trials. Did those bad guys really think they could get away with mass-murdering civilians? Every single person in the Empire might be an enemy of the New Republic. Each of the chief military representatives that actively sought to torture and kill innocent people would have to stand trial. Hence personal responsibility would be discovered during the Alderaan trials. Some of the commanders could be seen as innocent, but definitely not all of them.

Naturally the main antagonist could not be prosecuted (because he is probably dead), but we could move beyond legal liability, however important it is. The difficult query is about the role of institutional surroundings. What social scientists call "institutions" are broadly understood as "the rules of the game." They concern relations among people on all levels—starting with a family, moving on to a company, business relations, politics, laws, whole legal systems. Some thinkers are skeptical of overusing this word, and they are probably right to some degree. Perhaps it would be better to talk about a cultural framework and modus operandi, the habits of society.

Can we infer something about the rules of game in order to

understand how empires arise? You bet we can. Let's talk about those rules and their role in Palpatine's road to serfdom.

Start at the very beginning: the military side of the Trade Federation. As we established, having an invading army hardly suits a trade federation. It is perfectly understandable for any federation to have security measures, surely. There is a tremendous difference, however, between protecting trade routes and invading. Just look at what they actually possess: landing troops with tanks ready to comb the jungle and take over Naboo with total military backing. That does not really look like an efficient way of protecting trade. In other words, you can clearly recognize a difference between large defensive units (even well-armed ones) and a large, aggressive army. The Trade Federation is surely something other than just a trade organization, as it clearly has elements adapted to its political aspirations, including having soldiers to initiate aggression.

If only that was enough. Besides having a trained invasive army, they also have the legal power to levy taxes on market participants. Even if there are some legal rules defined by the Senate (as the quarrel with Chancellor Valorum indicates), the whole idea seems bizarre. How does an organization devoted to extending economic relations act as a state—with a monopolistic privilege to tax the people without their consent? Lawyers will tell you the main feature of the government: it can tax people, and it does that by building an apparatus based on physical force (army, police, courts, etc.). With that perspective in mind, we should not really treat the Trade Federation as an economic organization, but a sort of state: a political entity with a huge military and taxing power. Who gave them such extensive rights, and what is their moral authority?

The same problem arises when we consider the Galactic Senate. Galactic Senate, really? We do not have a world senate on Earth, which is populated by several billion people. Considering the creation of a world government, or world senate, leads almost anyone to shiver. With all the diversity on Earth, one can hardly imagine that a world senate and world government could govern a stable socioeconomic system.

Now multiply that problem a thousand times, both in the number of people and in the number of rationally-thinking species, plus hyperextend it geographically. A galactic senate and galactic government sounds much crazier than in case of an Earth government. No wonder such organizations ended up impotent and inefficient, highly corrupted, and focused mostly on lobbying schemes.

It's like the case of voting to give supreme powers to the chancellor. Everyone correctly points out that the vote was the end of the Republic. So why did they all take part in it? However, we should ask deeper questions: Why was there any possibility for such voting at all? Why was it at all possible to give anyone supreme powers? The problem was not just voting per se, but even the *potential* for doing so. That should not ever be an option in the first place. Just like how it should be questioned whether the Galactic Senate was needed at all.

Who gave military prerogatives to the Trade Federation? Who gave it taxing authority? Who undermined the right to self-determination of all the regions in the galaxy? Who came up with the idea of having one monopolistic government for all of the planets? Such questions can easily be multiplied, and we realize how badly the previous system was structured.

When we add everything together, we realize how dangerous galactic institutions are. The Trade Federation is a quasi-state igniting military and economic conflicts in order to reach the higher levels of unauthorized access to the chancellor's power. Such a body could be taken over by a madman, but its whole rationale for existence is questionable. Why should any planet care what those bureaucrats on Coruscant have to say about them? All the institutions create a volatile political mixture, a web of power that, carefully stimulated, leads to the rise of dictatorship. Those institutional surroundings are a necessity for a galactic dictatorship to arise.

Were it not for these favorable conditions, Palpatine would never have become the Emperor, and the First Galactic Empire would never have arisen. It is as much his fault as it is an institutional mistake. There would be no Order 66 secret service. There would be no massive genocide and galactic holocaust. There would be no Death Star and probably no Starkiller Base. Palpatine could merely become some hooded ruffian, an outcast menacing some place in the dark corners of Naboo using mumbo-jumbo about the Dark Side, probably stealing purses from the elderly, retired Gungans. Despite the necessity of it, Palpatine's evil is not a sufficient condition for dictatorship to arise. The political system had to pave a way for him to become the Emperor. Many of the obstacles must fall before he reaches his goal. And that is precisely the danger of the political system itself. We should fear the system itself much more than Palpatine. Why? Because there are hundreds of potential Palpatines out there in society. We should firstly make sure how to prevent them from monopolizing the government. We should close the road to serfdom rather than control every single person trying to walk it, because sooner or later our checks and balances may neglect another Palpatine.

Is There No Such Thing as the Light Side?

ONE thing particularly about the first six episodes of *Star Wars*—and not necessarily about *The Force Awakens*—grabs our attention. The first six episodes seem to reject what is known in philosophy as dualism (despite Lucas's intentions as expressed in interviews).

Did you ever wonder why we never get to hear about the Light Side like we hear about the Dark Side? In Episode VII, we hear something about "the Light," but it is marginal. Even during some of the extensive training rituals of the Jedi in the prequels, the Light never seems to come up. We have every reason to assume it is not a part of official Jedi vocabulary (I know, the books may have their own vocabulary, as does the excellent *Wookieepedia*). Most of the time though, throughout all seven episodes we hear about "the Force" and "the Dark Side of the Force." Whether or not the creators intended it, such phrasing implies that the Force and the Dark Side are not to be seen as true inverses. Yoda explains to Luke that the Dark Side is easier and faster and gives pleasing results, but comes at an ethical cost. In other words, the Dark Side is an aberration, not the inverse of the Force.

Which leads us in turn to the anti-dualist nature of *Star Wars* philosophy. Dualism views good and evil as equal opposites that are sometimes even complementary and reinforce each other. One cannot exist apart from the other, so they exist somewhat like twins who need each other. Some Eastern philosophies and religions rely on this sort of view, philosophies and religions whose traits are to be found in the Jedi philosophy. However, despite clear Jedi inspirations from Buddhism, the dualist concept—placing both good and evil on the same shelf—seems to be rejected in the original *Star Wars* story.

The Force is primary, it is natural, it is order, goodness, beauty, truth, and balance. The Dark Side, on the other hand, is a revolt against those things. It is chaos aimed at destroying balance to attain personal favors. The balance of the Force that Qui-Gon talked about does not mean the Force is balanced on the other side by the existence of the Dark Side. It means the Dark Side is to be wiped out completely, so only the true Force remains, without its Dark Side deviation. The mainstream of Christian religion has a similar understanding, as the evil, the Devil, is portrayed as a fallen angel—an aberration from the all-good God. It is not like in the movie *Constantine*, where two equal sides are fighting. The *Star Wars* story capitalized on that and—intentionally or not—rejected the dualist vision of forces of good and evil, despite clear and constant references to Buddhism.

The great writer C. S. Lewis eloquently rejected the dualist concept of good and evil as two equal sides:

> If Dualism is true, then the bad Power must be a being who likes badness for its own sake. But in reality we have no experience of anyone liking badness just because it is bad. The nearest we can get to it is in cruelty. But in real life people are cruel for one of two reasons—either because they are sadists, that is, because they have a sexual perversion which makes cruelty a cause of sensual pleasure to them, or else for the sake of something they are going to get out of it—money, or power, or safety. But pleasure, money, power, and safety are all, as far as they go, good things. The badness consists in pursuing them by the wrong method, or in the wrong way, or too much....

> You can be good for the mere sake of goodness: you cannot be bad for the mere sake of badness. You can do a kind of action when you are not feeling kind and when it gives you no pleasure, simply because kindness is right; but no one ever did a cruel action simply because cruelty is wrong—only because cruelty was pleasant or useful to him. In other words badness cannot succeed even in being bad in the same way in which goodness is good. Goodness is, so to speak, itself:

badness is only spoiled goodness. And there must be something good first before it can be spoiled.... [E]vil is a parasite, not the original thing.

In a similar way, the Dark Side is a spoiled element, a parasite on the Force, that cannot ever compare to the central idea of the Force.

The key thing about the Dark Side is that it is like a sin: it may appear anywhere, including within the Jedi themselves. We see this self-awareness with Yoda himself recognizing at least some of the mistakes the Jedi council made. The conflict depicted in *Star Wars* is not an evolutionary path drawn by two inverse forces: the Jedi versus the Sith. The conflict is between the Force as the original primary source of everything, and the Dark Side of the Force, which becomes an aberration, because people can spoil the Force. And the spoiling itself can be done by anyone, from any team. That is why caution is always necessary. Even when you think you are part of the non–Dark Side team, there is no guarantee you will not make a mistake. Hopefully, the opposite direction is possible, as we know from the father's conversion: one that chooses the Dark Side can always change their ways. The ending of *The Empire Strikes Back* changes the story from an adventure story of one side against the other to a redemption story.

Therefore, the heroes are not choosing between two inverse sides and teams. They are on a constant path to discovering the Force, which they can pervert, as they are susceptible to the Dark Side. This is a warning for everyone.

The Empire Awakens? Newer Trilogy and New Warnings

Most of this book has been devoted to the first six episodes of the *Star Wars* saga. The reason is obvious: there is enough material in those films to work with. The newest trilogy, which started with *The Force Awakens*, has yet to uncover a lot of what has happened since Palpatine fell into the abyss of space. (Or did he?) Various scenarios are possible, both on a personal level, and concerning what happened to the state apparatus after the fall of the Empire. We only have some scattered knowledge about the main character (Rey) and the assumed antagonist (Snoke). We have no clue what happened to Luke and what has happened to the post-Luke Jedi school. We do not know how the First Order came into being, or how it relates to the resistance movement and the New Republic.

The upcoming movie *The Last Jedi* may offer an interesting reflection on the issues discussed here. After all, the trailers reveal that Luke wants the Jedi to end. That sounds serious. As long as this is not some sort of movie-trailer Jedi mind trick, it could result from some of the problems we discussed above. Remember, Luke is the new wave of the Jedi. He rejected Jedi advice, he cherished life more, he was open to redemption and compassion—something even a ghost Jedi did not see. He was never trained according to the official rules. His mild defiance of many Jedi elements means he is also a Jedi reformer. Perhaps he is fed up with the older versions of the Jedi philosophy and understands why they failed in the past and therefore may easily fail in the future.

The questions about the post-Imperial evil guys are also interesting, although problematic. Remember, a monopolistic empire can do crazy and inefficient things just to demonstrate its power. For example, people know destroying a whole planet sounds like an idiotic thing to do even from the perspective of someone trying to be exploitative. But a Stalin-like dictatorship with full monopolistic force is capable of doing that. When dissolved into many smaller and weaker governments, such action becomes difficult, as the resources are much fewer and the power is diluted. In such a situation, someone can always question silly ideas: *Why should we destroy that planet? It may have valuable resources. Where do we get the funds to do that unprofitable thing?* Under the unified Empire, there could only be one Sith to rule them all. Everyone else shut up, or was quickly made to. Once the Empire fell like a house of cards though, resources must have quickly shrink, and power also. It will be interesting to see then how the First Order had the means to create a multi–Death Star machine, and how they all came to agree to get involved in such a meaningless act of destruction.

I do not really want to speculate about all this, as we just must give the creators some time and space to offer us more insights. In the context of the rise and fall of empires, the struggle is never completely over—especially since new generations must be brought up. Bad experiences are personal and not easily transmittable to the younger ones. You can listen to war veterans who do not talk proudly about the great warriors wars make. They tell you about the horrors of war instead. But no matter how hard they try, they cannot fully transmit their experiences to the new generation. Even if they devote a lot of time to it, and even if the new generation is interested, the experience stays personal. This is a sad reason why people commit the same mistakes over and over again: collective memory does not capture all bad experiences sufficiently. And so the rulers initiate wars again in later generations.

Similarly, an empire can rise again as the younglings develop sentiments about dangerous ideas of which they have very little understanding (one of the reasons you may still find Lenin's statue in Western countries even though he had millions of people killed). The new generation in the New Republic have never witnessed Darth Vader choking someone. They have not seen Tarkin's destruction of Alderaan. They have not seen how Palpatine terrorized the whole galaxy. The further we move away from the bad times, the higher the probability of moving back to them.

Bad ideas hardly ever die out. They go underground, they hide somewhere in the closet to wait for better times when they can lure newer people into foolish political systems. That surely is the warning we shall see, directly or indirectly, in the third trilogy.

EPILOGUE: MAY THE REASON BE WITH YOU

WELCOME to the final chapter. I've been waiting for you. We reach the end, at last. The circle is now complete. When we started, you were but the learner. Now, you are the master.

Some argue that *Star Wars* is a childish movie since it uses very simple art forms to communicate with the audience. But the forms should not blind us in searching for the content. *The Lion King*, for example, is a cartoon aimed at young audiences, but you can find a lot of valuable and serious propositions in it about society, power, corruption, seduction, and human relations. There is a Hamlet in the movie. I took a similar approach to the *Star Wars* movies and tried to find something valuable in them apart from a simple adventure story. Parts of them are clearly Shakespearean too, even the not-so-beloved dialogues between Amidala and Anakin, which were designed to be Shakespearean.

We can learn important lessons about the dangers of governments' power, and about their monopoly over various social institutions. We can learn about totalitarianism and what allows dictatorial regimes to exist. We can learn about effective checks and balances against those evils.

Who is the moral compass in *Star Wars*? The answer is different for each trilogy. In the case of the originals, it is an easier answer. Both Luke and Leia seem to fit the role (Obi-Wan and Yoda are not with us through the whole story, and there is something fishy about how they lie to Luke about Vader). But for the prequel trilogy, it becomes much harder, as no Jedi impresses us, and almost no politician. Amidala is the only sensible candidate, the one sane person in the room. I will take this chance to complain about her actions in Episode III. Not only does her talk about losing the will to live sound ridiculous, but her excusing of Anakin does much more. The original plan for her plotline was far better.

Do you remember that scene from Episode III that could have come from a soap opera? To paraphrase:

I'm so in love.

No, it's because I'm so in love.

In the original script, the scene ended with Anakin leaving the room and a representative of the separatists entering to conspire with Amidala. In that version, Amidala made the political reality much more complex by deciding that the separatists should be chosen over the imperialist Republic. More importantly though, she would conspire to eliminate Anakin Skywalker. Basically, she would know he is already morally problematic after having killed Sand People (the "hating Sand" reference may be a racist remark). That version would have been even better than the released version and would have been closer to Shakespearean drama: after finding out about Anakin's killing of the Jedi children, Amidala would have showed up with a knife in an attempt to kill Darth Vader on Mustafar (right before Vader's duel with Obi-Wan), making her character even more tragic. Too bad we did not end up seeing her in this light. The film makers decided instead to make her pacifist (and also not to portray separatists in a good light). That decision contradicted the first two episodes, where we clearly see her strength and sense of duty to always do the right thing. Despite her weakness in the third episode, she still is the best candidate for moral compass.

I guess the case for the filmmakers' writing her character the way they did was to show that she has the same compassion and forgiveness as Luke in his quest for redemption in *Return of the Jedi*. But they did so at a cost: we lost the compass of reason, which worked relatively well in the first two episodes. Yes, love indeed blinded her, not Anakin. Even so, she still has the faculty of critical thinking. It's something that should always guide every human being every day, especially in assessing important events like major political shifts, and something that should help people remember the dangers of power. Never admire power—even if it is "your people" that have it. So whenever you are tempted to use force against others because they are not from your team, resist it. You don't need to fall for this temptation. These aren't the methods you are looking for. Let the people go about their business.

Amidala embodies hope for future leaders, because she understands that in shaping social reality a leader has to serve the public, not the other way around; a leader does not make the public obedient and kneel before her. The prince of Lichtenstein, Hans-Adam II, a true, modern leader and the most democratic monarch of all time, expressed such a view in a book with the telling title *The State in the Third Millennium*:

> What kind of state does humanity want in the third millennium? President Kennedy, whom I had the honor to meet personally when I was a young man, said in his Inaugural Address in 1961: "Ask not what your country can do for you—ask what you can do for your country." As a young, idealistic person, I was in those days convinced by this statement. Today, I may not have lost all of my ideals, but decades of experience in national and international politics, including many years as the head of state of a small but modern democracy, have convinced me of the truth of the reverse statement: Ask not what a citizen can do for the state, but rather what the state can do better for the citizen than any other organization.

And that is the lesson of hope from *Star Wars*. Finally we can understand why it took place a long, long time ago, in a galaxy far, far away. Because hopefully it can be about our dark past, which we can safely leave behind us once we learn about the dark side of human nature. Because hopefully we will have less faith in the Hobbesian monstrosity on the cover of this book, and more hope for peaceful cooperation between all people.

Our romp with the *Star Wars* movies has reached an end. I believe that now you feel much more prepared to spot Sithian mind tricks. I assure you they are real.

I may have gone too far in a few places, but hopefully it has worked. May the Reason be with you.

INDEX OF NAMES

ABOUT THE AUTHOR

Mateusz Machaj is an assistant professor in economics at the University of Wroclaw (Poland). Besides his interest in technical economics, he works to increase public interest in the social sciences.